And is it True?

And is it True?

The case for Christianity

Stephen McQuoid and Alastair Noble

Authentic

10 09 08 07 06 05 04   7 6 5 4 3 2 1

First published in 2004 by Authentic Media
9 Holdom Avenue, Bletchley, Milton Keynes, MK1 1QR, UK
and
129 Mobilization Drive, Waynesboro, GA 30830-4575, USA
Website: www.authenticmedia.co.uk

British Library Cataloguing in Publication Data
A catalogue record for this book is available from the British Library

ISBN 1-85078-571-6

Cover Design by Sam Redwood
Typeset by WestKey Ltd, Falmouth, Cornwall
Print Management by Adare Carwin
Printed and Bound in Denmark by Nørhaven Paperback

And is it true? And is it true,
This most tremendous tale of all,
Seen in a stain-glass window's hue,
A Baby in an ox's stall?
The Maker of the stars and sea,
Became a Child on earth for me?

…

No love that in the family dwells,
No carolling in frosty air,
Nor all the steeple-shaking bells
Can with this single Truth compare –
That God was Man in Palestine
And lives today in Bread and Wine.

From 'Christmas'
by John Betjeman

To our long-suffering, wives
Debbie McQuoid and Ruth Noble

Contents

About the authors

Stephen McQuoid is the Principal of Tilsley College, Motherwell, which is part of the ministry of Gospel Literature Outreach. He teaches theology and evangelism at the college and has a preaching ministry that takes him throughout Britain and abroad. Along with his wife Debbie he is involved in a church planting work in Viewpark, Uddingston. This is his fifth book. He has also gained a DipTh in Theology, a BA and an MA in Biblical Studies, and is currently completing a PhD in Theology.

Alastair Noble, BSc, PhD, studied chemistry at the University of Glasgow. He has been a secondary school teacher, adviser, schools inspector and educational administrator. He has also worked, for short periods, on educational programmes within the BBC, the CBI and the Health Service. Since 2001, he has worked part-time as Field Officer for the Headteachers' Association of Scotland and Education Officer for CARE in Scotland. He is also a member of the Gospel Literature Outreach Team in Scotland and has undertaken occasional projects with Mission Scotland and the Billy Graham Evangelistic Association. In addition, he has had an extensive lay preaching and teaching ministry in the UK and overseas for many years. He lives with his wife Ruth, a primary school teacher, in Eaglesham and is an elder at Cartsbridge Evangelical Church in Busby, Glasgow. This is his first book.

Foreword

In the heart of the city of Glasgow lies the St Mungo Museum of Religious Life and Art. This temple to post-modernism contains a wide variety of artworks donated by the many religious communities that nestle within the cities boundaries. Its presence, right next to the cathedral, is a concrete expression of the values of our society. We now live in a culture where Christianity occupies no special place in the life of the nation. It is regarded as just one of many options open to people, and it competes in a crowded market-place with other world religions as well as with secularism.

Not far from Glasgow is Motherwell; in its heart lies the Gospel Literature Outreach Centre. This has been a haven of Christian witness for the past three decades. It is also the home of Tilsley College where we both teach. Obviously we are both committed Christians. But we are more that this. We also share the deep-seated conviction that Christianity is actually true. In essence this means that we are committed to believing in the uniqueness of Jesus Christ as the only Saviour of humankind, and believing that the Bible reveals what we need to know for faith and practice.

In the present intellectual climate, people who believe passionately in a particular truth, and believe it to be uniquely the truth, are often branded as intolerant and bigoted. However, because we believe that Christianity is an intellectually credible and coherent faith, we make no apology for our belief in its ultimate truthfulness. This book is an attempt to explain why we feel that this is the case. Essentially this book is a collection of essays, but these are connected to each other to produce one unit of thought which is our personal apologetic for what we believe.

Apologetics is a thoroughly biblical discipline. As we read through the book of Acts we often find evangelists like Paul reasoning with people and demonstrating the truthfulness of the gospel (Acts 17:16-31). Clearly, on these occasions, Paul was engaging in apologetics. We would also argue that 1 Corinthians chapter 15 is an apologetic for the resurrection. Furthermore, in 1 Peter 3:15, Peter states, 'Always be prepared to give an answer to everyone who asks you to give the reason for the hope that you have'. It is this desire to give an account of our faith that has prompted us to put pen to paper and write this book.

When a book reaches the market-place, there is no way of knowing who will end up reading it. But whoever you are, we hope that you will find it stimulating and interesting. If you are not a Christian but open to it, our hope is that this book will help you discover the truthfulness of the Christian message. If you are a Christian, we hope that it will affirm your faith. And if you are an ardent critic of Christianity or theism in general, we hope that it will at least give you pause for thought. We believe, from personal experience, in the reality of a God who saves, sustains and enriches our lives. We trust that this book will make some contribution to bringing this awareness into your life.

Stephen McQuoid and Alastair Noble

1

The big questions

Alastair Noble

I often wondered why the cabin lights on aircraft are dimmed for take-off and landing at night. I assumed it was either to save electrical power or perhaps to avoid reflections from the plane which could be misinterpreted by other pilots or control tower staff. Recently, on a flight, I asked a member of the crew about it and was quite surprised to learn that it is done because, if there had to be an emergency evacuation, the passengers' eyes would adapt more quickly to the darkness outside. Simple really, but the question had lingered in my mind for years because I felt my own explanation was not quite adequate. Actually I almost felt a bit more comfortable not knowing the answer!

If you don't ask, you'll never learn!

We are naturally curious. Listen to a young child ask questions and you can see how we learn. But adults are frequently too intimidated by the apparent knowledge of others to ask the question that troubles them. Or sometimes they are just too embarrassed to ask because they feel they are expected to know the answer. Often we settle for silent ignorance!

A regular criticism of our educational system is that it provides the answers before the students have asked the questions. Partly to deal with this, 'discovery learning' became fashionable in the 1960s and 1970s. Teachers were encouraged to create contexts in which pupils could ask the important questions and uncover the answers for themselves. A style of learning emerged which tried to capitalise on the inherent curiosity of young people. In more recent times, the Internet has allowed us to surf where we choose and find answers to our inquiries. But many of us still suppress our natural inquisitiveness, settling for the often sensationalised or trivialised information that is fed to us through the media.

Many really important discoveries were made because someone asked the right question. For example, the development of modern antibiotics, to which many of us probably owe our lives, came about by a chance observation and a thoughtful question. If you are ever in the vicinity of Paddington Station in London, you will easily find a plaque which identifies the laboratory at St Mary's Hospital where the Scottish researcher, Alexander Fleming, made the crucial discovery. Noticing by chance that the blue fungus which had grown on discarded samples killed the dangerous bacteria he was experimenting with, Fleming wondered what was happening. His persistence in trying to find an answer to the question which had arisen in his mind led eventually to the isolation of penicillin. A lesser scientist might never have made the observation or asked the crucial question!

Hard questions

It would be very surprising if this beautiful and mysterious universe we inhabit did not pose major questions to us. Where did it come from? Why is it here? Where is it going? What is the purpose of life? What is my personal part in it all?

At some time in our lives we all ask these kinds of questions. Once asked, they demand a satisfactory answer. Most of the time we are too busy just getting on with life to concern ourselves with such puzzles. But every once in a while our individual and distinct existence confronts us and leaves us feeling we need to know more.

In all human experience there is an unavoidable bottom line. The universe exists and we exist. They might not have existed and we would never have known, because we would not have been there to wonder about it! But once ultimate existence is glimpsed, however briefly and inadequately, it poses deep questions which never really go away.

Easy answers

There are, of course, plenty of confident and sometimes glib answers like the following. The universe started with a Big Bang. Energy solidified into matter. Life evolved by chance out of inanimate material. Life has no meaning. We are an accident of nature. We are destined for oblivion. Nobody can know what life is all about. There is no God. Religion is for intellectual dwarfs and emotional weaklings.

But no matter how confidently these positions are asserted, the mystery of the universe remains. It may be more comfortable to settle for tidy and undemanding answers but, somehow, none of them seems quite adequate for what our senses perceive all around us.

Someone once said that few things matter very much and most things don't matter at all. There is a good deal of truth in that. Our lives consist of hundreds of challenges and difficulties which, if you stand back from them, seem quite insignificant in comparison to the questions posed by the greater mystery of our existence. Trying to understand who we are and why we are here is surely among the few things that matter a great deal!

Surely science has cracked it!

It is understandable that, in our highly technological age, we expect the scientists to have found answers to the big questions of our existence. Certainly, there is no doubt that science has hugely influenced the modern world. It has given us antibiotics, aircraft, electricity, personal computers and a multitude of devices which have made our lives infinitely better than anything that could have been imagined a century or more ago.

Science has also given us some idea of the staggering dimensions of the universe. It has uncovered the huge distances in space which have to be measured in terms of the distance light travels in a year, moving at nearly 200,000 miles each second. Science has described the minute structure of molecules and atoms, each one of which, with its protons, electrons, neutrons and other subatomic particles, is as complicated as an entire solar system. It has elucidated much of the genetic code and begun to understand the complexity of the human brain. And if all this is not enough, it is claimed that the sum total of scientific information doubles about every ten years!

So you would expect science to have something substantial to offer in response to the questions at the heart of our existence. But, surprisingly, it has very little to say about these most fundamental matters. Science can give impressive insights into how nature works, but does not even begin to suggest why it is there at all. And yet, this is not really so surprising. Not when you consider the nature of scientific inquiry.

All scientific thought rests on the assumption that the universe is predictable and consistent. Why this should be so is an intriguing question in itself and suggests some prior cosmic decisions! If an observation or experiment yields a particular result today, we expect it to do the same tomorrow and the next day. If that was not the case, logical deduction would not be possible. Consequently, the development of any scientific theory, major or minor, involves a number of steps.

First, a series of observations is made by one or several people. Next, a suggestion or hypothesis is put forward to explain the findings. Then, if possible, a number of experiments are carried out to test the ideas which have been advanced. Finally, if the experiments confirm or modify the original suggestions, a general or wider theory is proposed. If any further experiment or observation calls the theory into question, the scientists have to think again and make the appropriate modifications to it!

Scientific theories, therefore, can never be absolute. They are always open to being adapted or contradicted by new findings. Professor Robert Winston, in a recent BBC Radio 4 programme, made the telling point that science is, ultimately, not about truth, but about uncertainty! The best scientific theories are the ones which minimise the degree of uncertainty. But none can ever remove it completely. And it is often forgotten, particularly in the debate about the origins of the universe and of life, that unless a scientific proposition can be tested and confirmed by direct experimentation or observation, it can never be more than a hypothesis or suggestion.

The boundaries of science

When you think about it, the limits of scientific inquiry are fairly obvious. For example, how would a scientist begin to measure human emotions like love or courage or anxiety? How does science explain the phenomenon of human consciousness? Or, more technically, how does science explain the ultimate nature of matter or energy and where they came from in the first place? Although it is not fashionable to stress the limits of scientific enquiry, it does science no service at all to pretend that it can pronounce authoritatively on matters which lie outside its method or about which it cannot possibly be certain.

When, occasionally, a prominent scientist pronounces that there is no God and that there is a straightforward mechanistic answer to the origin of the universe, he is simply going beyond the scientific method. Scientists may, for example, offer explanations of the processes by which life arose – and, as we shall see in later chapters, it is open to debate whether such theories are valid or not – but they cannot possibly know, by scientific inquiry alone, whether or not there is a Supreme Being who is the Architect of the universe. Science is definitely out of its depth here!

In this connection, it is worth noting that a great many scientists, both past and present, have been committed Christian believers. Among them are Galileo, Pascal, Newton, Faraday, Mendel, Pasteur and Kelvin. Of course, that does not, by itself, make Christianity true. But it does indicate that some eminent scientists have recognised the limits of scientific enquiry and found ultimate truth in other directions. And, in this connection, it is worth noting that the underpinning assumption of all science that the universe operates on predictable principles is largely derived from the historic Christian belief in the existence of one God who is the Originator of rationality!

Can the philosophers help?

Philosophy is another line of inquiry with a much longer tradition than science. It is, according to Brown, 'an intellectual activity concerned with the nature of reality and the investigation of the general principles of knowledge and existence'.[1] Every civilisation has had it philosophers who debated, with varying degrees of insight, the nature of the physical universe and human experience. A good deal of ancient philosophy is based on observations about the world which we would now consider to be invalid. Nevertheless, contemporary western thought still contains elements which come from ancient civilisations and, in particular, from the philosophers of Ancient Greece.

If science is the study of the natural world, philosophy is the analysis of human thought and ideas. Like science, its method requires rational thinking and logical analysis. It certainly produces disciplined mental activity and is a very powerful tool in the development of ideas. However, Brown argues that 'a good case could be made out for saying that there is no such subject today as philosophy. It is not a subject in its own right, such as chemistry, English, history, or modern languages. In the nature of the case it has no autonomous subject-matter. Philosophy is really always the philosophy of something else, whether it be the philosophy of science, the philosophy of history, or the philosophy of knowledge and communication. It has no private realm of its own'.[2]

So like science, philosophy has its limits. It is more an analytical tool than an absolute reference point. All philosophical ideas start with a proposition. Given a particular idea, philosophers can identify what it is reasonable to deduce from it. But the ultimate proposition that there is a God who created the universe presents a very special kind of intellectual challenge. Philosophy could accept the proposition and argue what must follow from it. It could also start from the nature of the physical and living world and argue towards the existence of a Creator. Equally, it could argue that there is no God and outline the logical consequences which flow from that view. But to pronounce on the absolute validity of either position would be beyond its method.

The limits of logic

The mystery which surrounds our universe underlines a fundamental feature of our existence. Logic and rationality determine the ways in which we think and make decisions. They are also powerful tools in unravelling the processes by which the natural world operates. But they appear to have very definite limits, beyond which we cannot progress. One biblical philosopher from 3,000 years ago, dealing with the apparent meaninglessness of life, provided a powerful summary of this intellectual dilemma: 'I have seen the burden God has laid on men. He has made everything beautiful in its time. He has also set eternity in the hearts of men; yet they cannot fathom what God has done from beginning to end.'[3]

The position is rather like looking across the sea to the horizon. We are certain about what we see up to the horizon and we are also sure that there is much more beyond it. But that lies beyond our visual capacity. Similarly, rational thought, whether in science or philosophy, appears to have a mental horizon beyond which we are unable to go, while all the time our instinct tells us there must be much more to life than we can explain.

How, then, can we ever know what appears to lie beyond the present reach of our minds? It is sometimes argued that as human beings learn more about the universe they will be in a better position to understand its origins and purpose. That may well be so. But it is more likely that there are aspects of our existence which will always lie beyond the capacity of our minds to unravel. The fact that the ultimate questions of our existence have been debated vigorously since the dawn of history makes that the more probable explanation!

Reason and revelation

Happily, there is a straightforward answer to the dilemma of our limited capacity to understand the nature of our universe. If Whoever or Whatever is beyond the reach of our perception chose to reveal what is there, we could know about it. The condition would be, of course, that we take such revelation on trust. Not surprisingly, this is what Christians have always called faith! Such faith need not contradict our rationality, but may well reach beyond it. Just as we might consider some event or incident to be 'supernatural' rather than 'unnatural', we could think of the Creator's self-revelation as 'super-rational' rather than 'irrational'! Faith would then involve the enlargement, not the abandonment, of our reason.

The Brilliant Watchmaker

In 1802, William Paley, an English theologian and tutor at Christ's College, Cambridge, made a simple but profound observation which continues to be a starting point for believers and sceptics alike. 'In crossing a heath, suppose I pitched my foot against a stone and were asked how the stone came to be there. For all I know, it might have been there forever. But suppose I found a watch upon the ground. Like any reasonable person, I would say the watch had been made by a watchmaker.' So, he concluded, a world needs a world-maker.

With all that we now know about our world, we are confronted with something infinitely more complicated than a watch mechanism! Michael Denton, a modern scientist, and not, so far as I am aware, a religious believer, makes this telling comment: 'It is the sheer universality of perfection, the fact that everywhere we look, to whatever depth we look, we find an elegance and ingenuity of an absolutely transcending quality, which so mitigates against the idea of chance. Is it really credible that random processes could have constructed a reality, the smallest element of which – a functional gene or protein – is complex beyond our creative capacities, a reality which is the very antithesis of chance, which excels in every sense anything produced by the intelligence of man? Alongside the level of ingenuity and complexity exhibited by the molecular machinery of life, even our most advanced artefacts appear clumsy. We feel humbled, as Neolithic man would in the presence of twentieth-century technology.'[4]

We would rightly reject the ludicrous notion that the millions of devices we use every day, from watches to airliners, have no designers or manufacturers and have simply appeared by chance. It is perfectly reasonable, therefore, to insist that a fully functioning and uncannily precise universe did not arrive by accident. The existence of an Architect for the universe – 'God' by definition – is as near to a self-evident truth as we are ever likely to encounter. Actually, the more challenging question about God is not whether he exists or not, but, what he is like.

The priority of faith

The answer of the Christian faith to all this is quite unambiguous. The 'good news' or gospel it proclaims is that we can know about God because he has chosen to reveal himself to us – not in every detail, of course, for a significant degree of mystery remains – but with sufficient clarity for us to make sense of our existence and to have a personal and functional relationship with our Creator. Such understanding requires that we accept what God has revealed – in his word, the Bible, and in his Son, Jesus Christ – and that we act upon it. The principle is stated in the Bible quite simply: '... without faith it is impossible to please God, because anyone who comes to him must believe that he exists and that he rewards those who earnestly seek him.'[5]

To accept, in faith, the self-evident existence of God and his self-disclosure is not an act of intellectual suicide or emotional weakness. Faith is not, as the eager Sunday school child once proposed, 'believing what you know isn't true'! On the contrary, it is believing what you know must be true. It is the only sensible response to the ultimate mystery of the universe.

In taking this step of faith we do not go *against* what is logical, but we certainly go *beyond* what logic is capable of establishing. Faith adds a further dimension to our understanding. One Bible writer summarises the nature of faith like this: 'Now faith is being sure of what we hope for and certain of what we do not see.'[6] That means faith completes the picture our mind constructs about the nature of God and the world he has created! After all, since God must be the Creator of rationality and logical thought, it's really not surprising that the nature of his existence lies somewhere beyond them.

Of course, you may not be inclined to accept, in faith, the existence of God and all that it implies. But what you

cannot do, in fairness, is to assert that the only intellectually acceptable position is that there can be no existence
beyond what can be rationally deduced. That smacks of
intellectual narrowness, if not arrogance!

When our children were small, my wife and I used to
worry about the few expensive ornaments we possessed.
It seemed the only two things the children were interested
in were whether they could be eaten or whether they
would bounce! So, we put the ornaments on a high shelf
beyond their reach. It does seem that our universe is
ordered in such a way that the answers to the most important questions lie just beyond the reach of rational analysis, but well within the grasp of faith.

A Christian world-view

So far, then, I have suggested that

- Existence and consciousness are profoundly mysterious phenomena.
- The beauty and complexity of the universe are well beyond the reach of chance and suggest that they are the
  product of intelligent design.
- Scientific achievement and philosophical analysis demand our respect, but both areas have definite limits.
- Scientific study and achievement is not incompatible
  with a strong Christian faith.
- We cannot reach God by our rationality alone, but with
  faith.

The Christian view of the universe is based ultimately on
what God has revealed about himself and about his activity in the world. That view will, of course, always be
informed by scientific and other discoveries. But it does
not concede final authority to any human conclusion,

however sophisticated, which is at best an incomplete picture of reality.

For a Christian, the ultimate truth about the universe and the life which exists within it is that God created them. It is also inescapable that Jesus Christ, whom Christians believe is the supreme revelation of God to the world, unambiguously endorsed that view. 'At the beginning the Creator made them male and female', he said.[7]

In summary, then, Christians believe that

- God is greater than anything we can conceive about him and any attempt to describe him is necessarily limited by our finite imagination.[8]
- The universe exists because God created it and it is a tangible expression of his unlimited power. The scale, variety and detail of the universe suggest that God's attitude to us will be reliable, predictable and personal.[9]
- Human beings were specially created by God. The physical universe has an awesome beauty and perfection, but it is essentially inanimate. Living things with their capacity to reproduce themselves are of a higher order. But human beings, with their capacity for conscious thought and productive relationships, are God's highest creative achievement.[10]

The Christian view is also that we are created by God to reflect something of his own existence. Charged with exploring, preserving and enjoying the wonders of this tiny but fascinating planet, we are, therefore, something rather special, rather unique! This is more a cause for humility and worship than for arrogance and pride. After all, we are not originals. We are, simply, made in the image of God.[11]

There is, too, in Christian teaching a more challenging truth. The confusion we often encounter in trying to understand the realities of our world can be to a large extent self- imposed. Indeed, it can be an escape from the moral consequences of acknowledging the existence of the Creator and his laws for our lives. If that is the case, we are significantly culpable before our Maker. St Paul sternly describes this phenomenon: 'For since the creation of the world God's invisible qualities – his eternal power and divine nature – have been clearly seen, being understood from what has been made, so that men are without excuse. For although they knew God, they neither glorified him as God nor gave thanks to him, but their thinking became futile and their foolish hearts were darkened. Although they claimed to be wise, they became fools ...'[12] So much for sophisticated agnosticism!

And there is a further principle. If we are made *by* God, we must also be made *for* him. Just as children depend on their parents or guardians for their protection and development, so we will not find lasting security and fulfilment in our lives until we reach out in faith to embrace the Creator's purpose for each of us.

The late Dag Hammarskjöld, who was Secretary-general of the United Nations, wrote in his 'Markings', 'I don't know Who – or What – put the question. I don't know when it was put. I don't even remember answering. But at some moment I did answer Yes to Someone – or Something – and from that hour I was certain that existence is meaningful and that, therefore, my life, in self-surrender, had a goal.'

There can be no doubt that God makes us sense his presence in the created order. But he goes much further. He reveals himself fully to us in his Son, Jesus Christ.[13] St Augustine, the great saint of the fourth century AD, understood this perfectly. Coming to faith after years of selfish and destructive living, he confessed, 'Our hearts are restless until at rest in Thee'.

Notes

1   Colin Brown, *Philosophy and the Christian Faith*, p. 8.
2   Colin Brown, *Philosophy and the Christian Faith*, p. 287.
3   Bible, Old Testament, Ecc. 3:10,11.
4   M. Denton, *Evolution: A Theory in Crisis*, p. 342.
5   Bible, New Testament, Heb. 11:6.
6   Bible, New Testament, Heb. 11:1.
7   See, for example, Bible, New Testament, Mt. 19:4-6.
8   See, for example, Bible, New Testament, Acts 17:24,25.
9   See, for example, Bible, New Testament, Col. 1:15,16;
    Heb. 11:3.
10 See, for example, Bible, Old Testament, Gen. 1:26,27;
    Ps. 8:1-9.
11 Bible, Old Testament, Gen. 1:26-30.
12 Bible, New Testament, Rom. 1:20-22.
13 See Bible, New Testament, Jn. 1:1-18.

2

Can meaning live when God is dead?

Stephen McQuoid

One of the most interesting lessons I have learned in the course of my life is the power of the conversation stopper. By that I mean the power that some subjects have to kill off a conversation. There are some issues that are so awkward, some subjects so unmentionable that if introduced at a social event, will often lead to a stony silence. Politics has traditionally been one of these subjects, particularly in countries where conflict is part of the culture. Death is another one and still another is personal hygiene. There are, however, few conversation stoppers so effective as the little three letter word GOD!

Once when visiting my parents-in-law, who live in the South Wales valleys, I went along to the Penygraig and District Philosophical and Debating Society. This was a pleasant gathering of locals who meet every Friday afternoon in a small room at the back of the second-hand bookshop in the village, to discuss and debate matters of mutual interest. The participants of this group were all well read and capable of arguing their case convincingly. Indeed the chair of the group had spent many years in Glasgow teaching in one of the city's major universities, as Professor of Medieval Archaeology.

I looked forward to the debate with considerable enthusiasm. As the chair spelled out the ground rules for the proceedings, he sternly told us that the only subjects which would not be admitted were politics and God. I found it interesting that the subject of God proved to be a conversation stopper of such magnitude that it was not allowed in this environment of apparent free speech.

This was no isolated situation. I have often found people embarrassed to talk about God. Whatever their world-view or belief system, many people prefer to push the subject of God to the back of their mind and keep it there. But whatever a person might feel about God, the subject of God is of utmost importance, not just for the promise of paradise, but also for this life. The existence of God is an essential element in that quest for true meaning in life. What is more, immortality, which is an attribute of God, is a quality that can enable a meaningful existence to be experienced.

Can meaning be found?

Many have asked the question, can I find meaning in life? This is because we, as human beings, need to feel that our lives count for something, that they are significant. It is linked to our self-esteem. To feel unimportant is to feel inadequate, and this is a difficult burden to bear. Enjoying a meaningful life is therefore a precious thing, and something that is worthwhile searching for.

A meaningful existence can be found when we look beyond ourselves to two other realities. Firstly, the reality of the existence of God, and secondly, the possibility of immortality.[1] These two realities can have a transforming effect on how we view our lives. In order to understand their significance, these two realities need to be viewed in both a negative and a positive way. From a negative point of view, if God does not exist, and if there is no possibility of immortality, then our lives would take on an austere and barren feel. However, if there is a God, and the possibility of immortality, our lives take on a huge significance that makes them ultimately meaningful.

We will look at the negative side of this equation first of all, by thinking of what the implications would be if there was neither a God nor the possibility of immortality. Just supposing there was no possibility of immortality. There was nothing beyond the physical realm that we now temporarily experience. The grave was our final destination and there was nothing beyond it. What would that say about our lives? Such a scenario would make the whole of humankind nothing more than a doomed race within a dying universe. There would be no hope for humanity. The human race would simply appear and then disappear. Every individual would exist and then pass into non-existence without having any control over their destiny.

A universe in which no possibility of immortality exists is one in which humans evolved by sheer chance with no reason for their existence, and then disappear in a similarly senseless way. If this was the case, then the question would need to be asked, what was the point of our existence in the first place? Would it ultimately have made any difference if mankind had never existed? Of course, on a personal level each of us would insist that our own lives are important or significant. But if we were to take a cold and rational view of the situation, why should we see our existence as any more meaningful than that of animals. After all, if like the animals we exist and then we die with nothing else in the equation, then in what sense is our life different from theirs?

We are capable of much more than animals. In terms of what we can accomplish we are undoubtedly superior.

But if our existence is simply snuffed out and we go into non existence with the same finality as animals do, if we like they become no more than a memory and then are ultimately forgotten about in this cold and vast universe, then why should we see our lives as ultimately more meaningful than theirs? In William Craig's own words, 'our life is not qualitatively different from that of a dog'.[2]

But even is there was the possibility of immortality, but no God to share it with, then what ultimate meaning would there be in this existence? Mere duration of existence is not in itself meaningful. Any prisoner serving a life sentence would confirm this. To live a life with no possibility of parole, and with no hope of escaping the tedium of prison life, would not make a prisoner look forward to more of those long years. In much the same way, if a person could live forever, but have no possibility of ascending to a higher plane and escaping the tedium of life, his existence would ultimately become meaningless. It would be like spending eternity going around in a revolving door that leads to nowhere better. Or perhaps like being stranded on a desert island surrounded by a vast ocean with no hope of getting back to the mainland.

Of course, many of us would argue that our lives are not tedious. On the contrary we spend time doing things that are interesting and absorbing. We enjoy leisure pursuits like the theatre, sports and an array of hobbies. We have our careers and ambitions which are of great importance to us. We enjoy our families and the relationships we have with our friends. All of these things combine to make our lives enjoyable and deeply fulfilling.

However, it must be stated that the enjoyment we have with these various aspects of our lives is attributed, at least in some measure, to the fact that we have not done these things for an eternity. They have been part of our lives for just a short time and so our capacity for enjoying them has yet to become frayed. However, if we were to have these things forever, if we were to live out the same existence indefinitely with no change, then their allure would eventually wear off. Our existence would become boring to say the least, and this would greatly detract from the meaningfulness of our existence. Only the existence of God and the possibility of knowing him could bring ultimate meaning to life.

Can value be found?

The problems that we would face in a universe with no God and no possibility of immortality are further compounded when we see the ongoing effects of this loss of meaning. This is because a loss of ultimate meaning would inevitably lead to a loss of value. If there was no God and no possibility of immortality, then there would also be no possibility of punishment for the wrongs committed in this life. After all, who would carry out the punishment of wrongdoers? And when would this punishment take place?

Such a situation would rob us of our motivation to do good! Why be good, with all the effort that can be involved in doing so, if there is no punishment for doing wrong? To use a bit of legal language, with no deterrent, why should we be virtuous? Why should we refrain from hurting others, if there is no one to answer to in the next life and therefore no repercussions to be faced? The word deterrent is not one that people warm to; nevertheless deterrents keep a society functioning for they impose a certain moral restriction on the harming of others. If a country had no prisons, no penal system, no police force and no method of dealing with crime, it would not be a utopia; rather it would be a lawless and chaotic society full of frightened and paranoid people. In much the same way, if there was no ultimate deterrent beyond this life, there would be no logical reason why people should not behave exactly as they wished irrespective of the consequences. A universe with no God and no immortality would be one in which there is no reason to do good to anyone. That being the case, what room would there be for values?

In any case, if there were no God, then how would we decide what was right and wrong? What decisions could be labelled as morally good or morally bad? We would simply have no objective basis for deciding moral issues. Crimes like rape and murder could not be condemned as being wrong. All that we could conclude is that some of us, as individuals, do not like these things or find them personally objectionable. But that would purely be our subjective opinion. Hitler could not be condemned for gassing six million Jews. We may not like what he did, indeed we might instinctively feel that his actions were obscene, but that would only be our opinion. Without a God to judge between right and wrong and to be a yard-stick against which all actions are judged, there is simply no objective way of saying what is right or wrong. Our whole system of morality would be relegated to the realm of subjective opinion. And, of course, different people would have different standards of morality which would lead to utter moral confusion. Only God can impose values on life. Therefore only the presence of God can establish an objective ethic.

The futility of existence

It goes without saying that if our existence is ultimately meaningless, and if we have no objective basis for morality, if there is no God to obey and no immortality to enjoy, then individual actions also become utterly futile. The scientist who toils day and night to find a cure for cancer or AIDS; or the UN peacekeeper, putting his or her life on the line to ensure that a ceasefire is maintained; their actions, though apparently virtuous and helpful on one level, are in fact ultimately futile and pointless. After all, any lives that they might manage to save would ultimately be lost anyway. In a sense they would not be saving life at all. Rather they would just be stalling the inevitable.

The scientist who discovers a cure for cancer would enable sufferers to exist for a few more years, but ultimately they would die anyway of some other cause, and then they would end up in extinction. The same is true for the UN peacekeeper, standing between two warring factions in order to prevent them from killing each other. The peacekeeper would save the needless slaughter of innocent people, but those whom they save are doomed anyway and will inevitably die and go into extinction, irrespective of what the peacekeeper does. It is really only a matter of time. As the efforts of these two people would lack any objective moral content anyway, and their effects are only temporary, the question might well be asked, why bother? In reality, if this is the kind of universe in which we live, if there is no God and no possibility of immortality, then the only sensible way to live is to be utterly selfish and self-serving, and to enjoy our existence while we can, because soon it will be taken away from us.

Having thought about meaning, values and futility, it is reasonable to conclude that without the existence of God and the possibility of immortality, human beings are nothing more than animate matter that came about as a result of a sheer mindless accident, with no reason or purpose to their existence. As humans we would therefore be insignificant people living ultimately meaningless lives. It is conceivable of course, that this might possibly be the case, but it would be an existence so unbearable that that it would render the whole universe a senseless waste of time and energy.

Many people realise this, at least on a subconscious level. Though they might not have any specific or even correct beliefs about God, they instinctively feel, and hope that there is some controller or divine being behind the universe ensuring that everything does not fall into chaos. At whatever level this belief exists, it is an important one at least in as much as it enables people who are not necessarily religious to nevertheless maintain their sanity and have a confidence that there is some order to the universe. In this sense humankind desperately needs there to be a God and the possibility of immortality for, without God, life would simply be absurd.

God + Immortality = real meaning and value

Of course, if we were to take the position that God does indeed exist, and that there really is the possibility of immortality, then the situation is altogether different. If we look at these two realities from a positive perspective we find ourselves in a very different kind of universe. The universe we would inhabit would be one where absolute ethics could exist because we would be able to learn them from God. These ethics would be objective and unalterable as they would not depend on human whim or opinion. It would also be a universe in which justice could be a reality for there would be someone who could punish wrongdoing and even reward those who do what is right. This justice would in turn produce constraints on human behaviour because of the repercussions which wrongdoing would attract, and the deterrent of judgement. More than that, it would be a universe in which people would be

inspired to do things which were positively good and con-
structive because there were moral reasons for doing so.
And if immortality were also a reality then these good acts
could be rewarded with an endless life of reward.

If God is real and if there is such a thing as immortality,
then this is the very best thing for humankind. For it
makes life worthwhile and enables good to exist. If people
within our society were convinced of the existence of God
and of the possibility of immortality, that belief in itself
would make its mark on the way we as a society choose to
live. Clearly therefore, much is at stake. Whether or not
God exists is not just a subject for debate, it is an issue that
can transform society.

Notes

1   A useful exploration of these two realities can be found
     in the excellent book by William Lane Craig, *Apologetics:
     An Introduction*, pp. 39-36. This chapter is indebted to his
     work.
2   William Lane Craig, *Apologetics: An Introduction*.

3

Is there really someone out there?

Stephen McQuoid

We need God! That much is clear. If anything is to be learned from the previous chapter it is that if there is no God, and no possibility of immortality, then life is absurd. And if anything is to be learned from the first chapter it is that the existence of God provides answers for our most fundamental questions about our existence and that of the universe. But does God actually exist? After all, it does not necessarily follow that if we need something then it must therefore exist.

Asking does God exist is as fundamental a faith question as anyone can ask. Certainly it is the most basic question of Christian apologetics. It goes without saying that if there is no God then any attempt to defend the Christian faith would be utterly meaningless. Faith can only be real if it is based on something. We need therefore to think of the evidences for God's existence.

From a personal standpoint, I can attest to the reality of God's presence in my life and this certainly affirms my Christian faith. But personal testimony will not always impress those who are naturally disposed to be sceptical about faith or religious belief. This is particularly true when those same people have heard testimony from people who adhere to other belief systems. I have often been asked the question 'Why is your testimony more valid than that of other people?' This question is both fair and logical. While I would not deny the veracity of my testimony, I would nevertheless recognise the need for coherent and logical reasons for the existence of God. These reasons need to be objective rather than subjective, and built on the foundation of shared reason and logic. By this I mean that the logic of the argument is such that others can see it, not just me.

Throughout human history there have been a number of different arguments put forward for the existence of God. Some of these have proved highly convincing and have therefore been used effectively in defending theism. These arguments have been refined and restated by different generations of Christians using a variety of different analogies. We will look at some of these arguments and use some analogies that will help us to explore them.

Argument from cause

The first argument for the existence of God is a very simple one, yet profound. This is the argument based on the need for a cause. Put simply, it works on the premise that everything that exists must have a cause for its existence. Things cannot simply exist uncaused. They must attribute their existence to something else outside of themselves.

This process of cause and effect cannot keep going back forever. At the end of the line there must be something, or someone, who causes everything else to be caused, but which is uncaused. That thing, or rather person, by definition, is God.

There are a number of analogies that can be used to illustrate the argument from cause. One useful analogy is that of a train and its carriages. If you see a train carriage moving along, you would not conclude that it is pulling itself. The reason for this is that you know that carriages have no engines; they are therefore not able to make themselves move. To use a philosophical expression, they cannot actualise their own potential. But then you see another carriage attached to the first one and you realise the obvious. The initial carriage is being pulled along by the second one. But once again you don't assume that this carriage is pulling itself for much the same reason. It is no more capable of moving of its own accord than the first carriage, for it too lacks an engine. You then see several more carriages, all attached to the first two and all moving. Ultimately, you will expect to find an engine which is pulling all these carriages. This is the only feasible explanation for the movement of the carriages. And when you see the engine you no longer need to assume that it is being pulled by something else, because you know that it has the ability to pull itself along. This engine causes the carriages to move but is itself uncaused. This is the argument from cause, or the cosmological argument.

This argument can easily be used as evidence for the existence of God. The universe owes its origins to something. It is irrational just to assume that it was always there and did not require a cause. It could not have just happened. There must have been a cause that brought it into existence. And like the train, the succession of causes cannot go back indefinitely. There must ultimately be a cause which was in itself uncaused. A mover who is unmoved, or to put it another way, a Creator who is uncreated. That ultimate cause is God.

Of course, many people would argue that this is an assumption, that there are other explanations for the universe other than that of a Creator God. Perhaps the most significant of these is the theory of evolution that was first popularised by Charles Darwin, and is now being championed by scientists such as Richard Dawkins. The interface between science and belief will be dealt with later in this book, but for now, we need to note that the theory of evolution does not satisfy the requirements of this argument from cause. I will illustrate this by mentioning a conversation that I had some years ago with a committed evolutionist.

The person in question was called Karl (not his real name) and I met him in Copenhagen. Early on in our conversation he told me that he was an atheist and that he felt that evolution was the most credible explanation for the existence of the universe. I in turn told him that I was a theist and that the argument from cause demanded that there be a Creator. He, of course, disagreed. So I asked him where man as a species came from. He replied by stating that man had essentially come from the ape. Then I asked where the ape came from to which he replied that in a long process of events the ape came from primordial slime that emerged from the water which covered the earth. 'So where did that come from?' I asked. 'Well,' he said, 'the earth appeared and took shape after the Big Bang which was caused by complex gases colliding in the universe.' I then asked where the complex gases came from. He stated that they formed after some more primitive gases were mixed. Still persistent I asked, 'Where did the primitive gases come from?' His reply was, 'I don't know, they were just there.'

The problem with his argument was that it simply did not explain the presence of matter. It kept working back to other causes, but it did not go back to an uncaused cause: Some kind of force which made everything else happen but which was itself uncaused; a creator who was uncreated. For the theist this is not an issue for God fulfils the role of the uncaused cause.

Argument from design

Another argument which is compelling is the argument from design. This argument has already been alluded to in chapter 1, but it is such a significant argument that it deserves repetition. The argument from design is sometimes referred to as the teleological argument. Again the basic idea behind this argument is simple, but nevertheless powerful. It works on the assumption that in order for such an intricately designed universe to exist, there must be an intelligent designer behind it. This argument is not so much about the actual fact of the existence of the universe, but rather about the nature of the universe.

This argument from design was used effectively some two hundred years ago by William Paley. His method was to amass evidence within the natural order. This included bones, muscles, blood vessels and other organs throughout the animal kingdom. He would demonstrate just how intricate these things were, and in turn, how intricate the universe in which we live is. He would then demonstrate the necessity of a designer through analogy.

Paley used the analogy of a watch, something that is very much simpler than the universe.[1] He reasoned that if he came across a watch lying on the ground and inspected it, his conclusion, even if he had never seen a watch before, would be that it was something designed by an intelligent being rather than something that just happened to be there. Indeed to assume that this watch simply appeared as a result of blind forces, time, matter and chance, would be utterly illogical. He would reach this conclusion because the watch had many gears and a spring that worked together to make the hands move in perfect coordination with each other. It thus demonstrated design.

Paley then argued that if it was logical to conclude that something as simple as a watch was designed, and therefore had to have a designer, then the universe that is infinitely more complex, and demonstrates much more sophisticated coordination, also has to have a designer. Though Paley's argument was simple, it was nevertheless compelling. When we look at some of the intricacies of the universe and realise how tremendously complex it really is, the idea that it just happened and came together merely by chance is simply stretching the bounds of credibility. Even if you allow for a great deal of time as evolutionary science suggests, there is still no logical reason to suggest that an ordered and complex universe can emerge from some sort of primeval chaos without the presence of a purposeful and intelligent designer. It would be a bit like blowing up a scrap yard, leaving it for a long time, and then expecting to find a perfectly assembled jumbo jet at the end of the process. This kind of order simply doesn't happen by chance. In much the same way, a complex universe logically requires there to be an intelligent designer. That designer is God.

Moral argument

Another line of argument which is compelling is the argument based on the innate sense of morality that human beings seem to possess. Human history is littered with terrible atrocities which demonstrate evidence of humankind's inhumanity to humankind. But there are also many accounts of noble self sacrifice for the benefit of others. In addition, a great many people believe in the concept of morality, and they honestly endeavour to live the best lives they can. They do not just react instinctively to situations, but have a definite sense of what is right and wrong.

The question is, where does this nobility, or sense of morality come from? Why do we have an inbuilt sense of what is right and wrong, and why do we allow this to guide our actions? After all, this cannot simply be explained by evolution. If we were merely the product of chance and mindless forces then we would only act according to our survival instinct. We would not be able to feel that something was right or wrong, true of false. Neither can it be explained by mere environmental conditioning since it occurs in the lives of people from every culture and background, though not necessarily in a uniform way.

If the average person in the street were to be asked to comment on the Holocaust, or the actions of the Yorkshire Ripper, he would immediately say that these were very evil acts. He may not know the basis on which he makes these moral assertions, but he would instinctively know they were wrong, and would probably feel very strongly about it. Where does this sense of outrage come from?

It seems as if the most credible answer is to accept the existence of a moral Creator who instils in us, his creatures, a sense of morality. This idea of God as Creator, making us moral, is precisely what the Bible claims.

I remember having a conversation some years ago with a secular Jew. As we talked he insisted that my belief in God was misplaced. Though Jewish, he had no assurance that there was a God or that his religious tradition provided any real justification for theism. Rather than get into a deep philosophical debate, I simply asked, 'What do you think of Adolf Hitler and his treatment of your fellow Jews?' Understandably he got annoyed; this was a very sensitive issue even for a secular Jew. 'He was evil,' was his response. I then asked him why he felt that way. He replied by stating that anyone who would butcher so many innocent people must be incredibly evil. At this point I asked him to prove to me that he had a concrete basis by which he could condemn such acts of barbarism.

He had to admit that as long as he denied the existence of God he would not be able to, but he nevertheless felt strongly that it was wrong. All I had to do then was to point out that his strong and undeniable sense of morality was itself evidence of the existence of a moral Creator who gives his creation a sense of morality. In other words the existence of God.

Notes

1   For a detailed description of Paley's argument see W.L. Craig, *Apologetics: An Introduction*, p. 68.

4

Whatever happened to Darwin?

Alastair Noble

You may have noticed the row that broke out in 2003 over the claim that creation was being taught alongside evolution in a new style Christian secondary school in Gateshead in England. The chorus of condemnation from scientists, educationists and bishops, including a piece on BBC Radio 4's 'Thought for the Day', was impressively orchestrated. One voice called for school inspectors to be sent in without delay and later described the approach as educational debauchery. To merit such a rapid and almost rabid response you would have thought that something on the scale of Nazism or Apartheid was being propagated. But creationism? Is it that dangerous? And no one thought to mention the hugely impressive results being achieved by the school in national examinations with pupils from areas of significant social deprivation. It left the unmistakable impression that someone had kicked a sacred cow!

Big ideas

Most of us recognise a good idea when we see one. But only very few ideas have changed the course of history. For example, the construction of the first wheel thousands of years ago must have revolutionised transport dramatically. The erection of the first stone arch centuries ago radically altered architecture. The discovery of electricity in the nineteenth century was arguably the single most important contribution to the development of the modern world.

But not all big ideas have had such beneficial results. The experiments which suggested that matter consists of tiny atoms were carried out around the beginning of the twentieth century. But barely fifty years later, by the end of the Second World War in 1945, that discovery had led to the use of the first atomic bomb, with devastating results for the population of two Japanese cities and huge uncertainty for the future of the world.

Without doubt, one of the most pervasive ideas of modern thought is the theory of evolution and its application to the origin of life. It is now not only taught at every level of our public education system as an indisputable scientific fact, but is regularly invoked as the basis for sociological and political trends which lie far beyond the field of natural science. Evolution is regarded by some as the most fundamental principle of the universe. To challenge it, or even to consider an alternative view of origins, is to incur the immediate scorn of the educational and, sadly, of parts of the religious establishment. It is salutary that an evolutionist of the stature of Stephen Jay Gould, writing about the power of a well-chosen picture, has observed the danger that 'ideas passing as descriptions lead us to equate the tentative with the unambiguously factual.'[1]

So how did evolutionary thought get this dominant position? The idea that the universe evolved out of nothing and that life arose from non-living material goes back a very long way. But in its modern form, the theory of evolution goes back to the mid-nineteenth century and especially to the work of the natural historian Charles Darwin.

Darwin the doubtful

As a young man, Charles Darwin studied medicine and prepared to enter the service of the church. But neither of these routes opened to him: the former because he soon lost interest; the latter because he eventually lacked faith.

In the 1830s the opportunity to be the naturalist on HMS *Beagle*, a scientific survey vessel, was to prove irresistible to the inquisitive Darwin. His best known work was done in South America and in the Galapagos Islands off the coast of Ecuador. These islands, some six hundred miles from the mainland, provided unusually isolated breeding grounds for a large number of plants and animals and it was there that Darwin made some of the key observations on which the modern theory of evolution is based.

It is an intriguing irony that Darwin's work was to become such a challenge to the doctrines of the church he had once hoped to serve. It is also interesting that Darwin agonised significantly over the accuracy of the conclusions he drew about the origins of life and their implications for Christian doctrine. Robert Clark describes how, 'One moment he thought he could do without design; the next, his reason told him that the evidence for design by a personal God was overwhelming. He was for ever seeking an escape from theology but never able to find it.'[2]

What the biologist saw

So what did Darwin actually see? At the risk of hugely oversimplifying, you could say that what he noticed, both from the fossils and living things he studied, was that

- within a given species or type of living thing, wide variations in form and fine detail are possible, and
- that groups of creatures with certain specific characteristics survive in certain environments but not in others.

So, for example, within populations of birds or turtles, there were small, but very noticeable differences within the groups which inhabited different islands. For turtles, one difference might be in the pattern of their shells. For birds, it might lie in the length of their beaks. And you can see how this could be important. For birds, short beaks might be fine if the food required is readily available. But if the birds had to dig for it, then short beaks could be fatal and longer beaks become essential. It is fairly obvious, then, that animals with certain characteristics will survive in one type of environment but not in another.

Expanding evolution

The impressive variety of the living creatures Darwin studied and the many small but intriguing differences he noted between very similar types led him to think about how all this could have arisen. He called the process by which animals with certain characteristics persisted in some environments, but not in others, 'natural selection' or the 'survival of the fittest'. Only those creatures which are specially suited to a given environment will survive. The others will simply die off because they lack the ability to survive in that environment. This he came to believe, was a fundamental principle of nature. He was eventually to publish his ideas in *On the Origin of Species by means of Natural Selection* in 1859.

Darwin believed that this 'natural selection' provided the driving force for the two other major processes he thought had affected the course of nature. These were that, firstly, the different species of animals and plants which we now recognise are not fixed and that new varieties have appeared over the long history of the earth; and, secondly, that the very wide diversity of life has arisen by the process of evolution from a small number of common ancestors.

Darwin's ideas have, of course, been greatly developed since his time and are now presented in the much more sophisticated form of Neo-Darwinism. But the basic conclusions remain essentially the same. It is now almost universally accepted that given enough time – and billions of years are suggested – simple living things will evolve into more complicated creatures. And the ultimate step in the evolutionary hypothesis has also been taken: if evolution is the underlying principle in generating the full range of living things, it could also be the means by which life itself emerged from non-living matter. The extent to which such thinking has become embedded in our culture is evidenced by the recent excitement about the new evidence that there may be life on Mars. What is it that has been discovered? Actually, just some data to suggest that there may be ice on the Red Planet. Rather a long way away from real life in any shape or form!

And so, from a series of observations in a handful of far-away islands, a beautifully simple principle was thought to have been discovered, with the potential to offer an explanation for the origin of the universe and everything in it. Not bad, you might say, for a mid-nineteenth century round-the-world cruise by a not very well-known biologist!

Inevitably, the need to recognise the existence of a Creator of the world has been called into question. Darwinism became, as he himself feared, a direct challenge to theism and to the Christian view of creation. Evolution quickly came to be regarded as the creative principle of the universe and the challenge was, and still is, to find as much evidence as possible to substantiate its claims. Some would argue, of course, that Darwinism and Christianity are not incompatible. But, in popular understanding, evolution effectively disposes of religious beliefs about the origins of the universe. It appears to provide, after all, what the modern world likes best – a neat, tidy and materialistic explanation with no uncomfortable moral implications. But is it that simple?

Then came DNA

Darwin, of course, had no knowledge of DNA or, for that matter, of the basic principles of genetics. He proposed that living things could acquire new characteristics through natural selection, but he was understandably vague as to how that came about. Mendel's systematic cultivation of different kinds of peas, from which he was able to deduce the existence of dominant and recessive genes and lay the foundations of modern genetics, was to come some years after Darwin's work. The elucidation of the structure and some understanding of the chemistry of DNA, that beautifully complex, double-helical molecule which carries all the coded information living things require to reproduce themselves, was not achieved until the 1950s and later.

We now know that living organisms are complex, almost beyond belief. A single living cell contains many thousands of complicated substances – proteins, sugars, fats, enzymes and hormones, to mention only a few – and these are constantly involved in an endless series of biochemical reactions. Some release the heat and energy our bodies need to function properly; others carry vital messages to the brain and nervous system; and still others regulate the acidity levels of the blood and body fluids in order to hold them within the very narrow limits required for life and health. And the average human body has something of the order of ten trillion of these cells!

It is also astonishing that each cell of our bodies carries a full set of DNA with genetic material coded exactly to give the set of characteristics which are unique to each of us. Someone has calculated that if all the molecules of DNA in a human body were joined together in a single strand – much too small to see of course – it would reach to the moon and back, 8,000 times!

You may argue that there is not much significance in such a calculation. But at the very least, it underlines the immense complexity of the genetic material within our bodies. Since it only requires the DNA from a single male sperm and from a female egg to provide the complete blueprint for a new human being, you have to wonder at the intricacy of the genetic information which is coded on its molecular structure. That such sophisticated information, carried in substances within cells which we cannot even see with the naked eye, should arise as a result of blind chance or mindless processes stretches credulity beyond the limit. The complexity of the information carried in DNA demands a more satisfying explanation and points to the awesome possibility that it is there by deliberate and intelligent design.

For modern evolutionists, Darwin's inherited characteristics require a biochemical explanation and it is not easy to see what it is. The small changes which can occur in DNA under the influence, for example, of certain chemicals or radiation – 'mutations' as they are called – or just by biochemical 'accidents' seem the most obvious route. But while a mutation could occasionally bring about a beneficial change in the genetic code, it is much more likely to be destructive. In practice, mutations are much more likely to produce cancer than increase complexity! And to argue that random mutations can be responsible for generating the vast complexity of the genetic code is a bit like saying that spraying shotgun pellets into a china shop will sooner or later produce a Ming Vase! Some things are just inconceivable! And, of course, even if it was possible to increase the complexity of the information carried in DNA by the process of mutation, you are still left with the problem of how DNA got there in the first place.

A different perspective on origins

There is, then, another view which is certainly worthy of consideration and which, to an increasing number of people who think seriously about the issue, is compelling. Stated simply, it is that the existence of DNA, the genetic code and all the information it contains suggests strongly that there has been intelligent design. And intelligent design indicates that there is a Creator's hand behind it. If that is so, the complexity and sophistication of the genetic code is quite deliberate. Just as many modern computer program contain a large range of applications, many of which the average user never employs, so it is not hard to believe that 'designed DNA' will contain a vast array of possibilities.

Instead of postulating that the variety of life must have built up over huge periods of time by vague and rather ill-defined evolutionary processes, we can visualise it deriving from original sets of genetic information into which all the possibilities had been deliberately and intelligently embedded. Far from being a crude creationist assertion, that view is a much more credible proposition. And it would not be necessary to postulate that vast periods of time are necessary for the emergence of the full range of living things. It does, however, accept that life is no accident and is the direct result of a Creator's activity. This explanation of origins cannot just be dismissed because it dares to go beyond purely materialistic explanations.

Surely fossils fix it!

Just about everyone who has taken a biology course at school or at university has been led to believe that the existence across the world of a large variety of fossils of everything from shells to dinosaurs, provides the ultimate evidence for evolution. That this is very far from the case, as a number of recent writers have pointed out,[3] is not generally publicised. A few textbooks, however, recognise the tenuous nature of the evidence from fossils. For example, one textbook which was popular in Scottish secondary schools in the 1980s, in its treatment of the fossil evidence acknowledges that a different interpretation, which does not lend support to the theory of evolution, is possible.[4]

It certainly comes as a bit of a shock to discover that much that is claimed for the fossil record is open to question. For example, it is normally assumed that fossils have been laid down slowly and steadily by processes which have continued uninterrupted for millions of years. But another possible explanation for the creation of fossils, or at least a substantial proportion of them, is that large numbers of living things were caught up in catastrophic events – perhaps similar to the volcanic destruction of Pompeii in the first century or the great floods of antiquity – and buried very quickly and completely. There are also some grounds for believing that the dinosaurs, of whom we have many fossils, died out very rapidly as a result of a cataclysmic event, perhaps involving the collision of the earth with a meteor or comet. The fossil record might point just as readily to a stormy and turbulent past for our planet!

Another widespread assumption is that the fossil record contains the 'missing links' or transitional forms required by evolutionary theory. But such a proposition is hard to substantiate and their absence has been, from Darwin's time, a significant embarrassment to evolutionists. The fossil record certainly contains the remains of many types of creatures, some of which have only minor differences from each other. But genuine transitional forms remain highly illusive. A more credible interpretation of fossils is that they display the endless variety living things can generate – a conclusion which is not the same as arguing that one species evolved into another.

It is also sometimes claimed that the fossil record contains a steady progression from simple organisms to complex creatures. But that is a fairly selective view. Sections of the record show quite confusing patterns, such as the 'sudden' appearance of certain creatures without any obvious predecessors or the presence of very different types in the same strata of rocks. A further complication is that the dating of the particular fossils is often dependent on a number of assumptions about the age of the rocks in which they appear.

The interpretation of the fossil record is, therefore, determined to a significant extent by the presuppositions brought to it and it does not provide indisputable evidence for evolution. Indeed Darwin himself conceded that fossil evidence was 'the most obvious and gravest objection which can be urged against my theory'[5] and the problems he saw are far from being removed. Hardly, then, the clinching argument for evolution! Phillip Johnson is uncomfortably close to the reality of the situation when he claims that 'if evolution means the gradual change of one kind of organism into another kind, the outstanding characteristic of the fossil record is the absence of evidence for evolution.'[6]

So is evolution credible?

Well, in fairness, it all depends what you mean. If by evolution you mean the phenomenon that, over time, groups of living things adapt to their environments by the natural selection of those best suited to them, then there is no doubt that evolution is a property of life. This is essentially what is known as 'microevolution'. It recognises that the genetic code of all species carries within it a wide range of possibilities and, over several life cycles, the offspring with the characteristics best suited to their surroundings are most likely to survive. They are also the ones, by the principles of genetic inheritance, most likely to produce further offspring with the features necessary for survival. You could argue that without that capacity, any living creature would not persist beyond a few generations.

If, on the other hand, you take evolution to mean an all-embracing universal process by which living things emerged from inanimate material and progressed over huge periods of time from simple organisms to complex creatures – generally known as 'macroevolution' – then there are substantial grounds for doubt.

Macroevolution is by its very nature untestable and requires huge trust in the blind forces of nature. Indeed, such are the difficulties in sustaining this position that a view taken by some is that it would only be possible if a Creator chose to direct it in this way. That may sound like a sensible conclusion, but, for the true materialist, it has the ring of admitting defeat! This wider theory of evolution is often defended essentially from the point of view that it must be true because there is no other credible explanation – unless you admit to a Creator of course!

Some scientists recognise the immensity of what is being proposed in macroevolution. Francis Craik, the celebrated co-discoverer of DNA and Nobel Prize winner, has expressed the view that, 'An honest man, armed with all the knowledge available to us now, could only state that in some sense, the origin of life appears at the moment to be almost a miracle, so many are the conditions which would have had to have been satisfied to get it going'.[7] He has even gone so far as to suggest that life may have originally been seeded on earth from space,[8] a position which leads Michael Denton to comment, 'Nothing illustrates more clearly just how intractable a problem the origin of life has become than the fact that world authorities can seriously toy with (this) idea.'[9]

A few scientists are beginning to express the view that evolutionary science does not provide a wholly convincing position on origins.[10] Some go further and even suggest that evolutionary science is bad science. And they are certainly not arguing from the position of religious belief. Michael Denton, the author of a powerful critique of evolution which he describes as 'a theory in crisis', is one of them. His conclusion, based on a detailed examination of evolutionary theories in areas such as molecular biology and palaeontology, is staggering but fair. 'Ultimately,' he writes, 'the Darwinian theory of evolution is no more or less than the great cosmogenic myth of the twentieth century.' And he concludes, 'The truth is that despite the prestige of evolutionary theory and the tremendous intellectual effort directed towards reducing living things to the confines of Darwinian thought, nature refuses to be imprisoned. In the final analysis we still know very little about how new forms of life arise. The "mystery of mysteries" – the origin of new beings on earth – is still largely as enigmatic as when Darwin set sail on the *Beagle*.'[11] This kind of humility in the face of the sheer complexity of natural systems is refreshingly honest.

A new authoritarianism

Richard Milton, a scientific journalist, takes the whole matter a stage further. In his book, *The Facts of Life*, subtitled 'Shattering the myths of Darwinism', he insists that the 'tacit consensus' that it is bad form to criticise science or scientists in any way needs to be challenged. He writes: 'I am a customer for the scientific service that we pay the scientists to provide, and I have a complaint: I am not satisfied with the answers they have provided on the mechanism of evolution and I want them to go back to their laboratories and think again.' And he continues, 'There is a strong streak of intellectual arrogance and intellectual authoritarianism running through the history of Darwinism ... This authoritarian streak is still present in some Darwinists today and is denoted by the outrage and indignation with which they greet any reasoned attempt to expose the theory to debate and to the light of real evidence.' He advocates that such authoritarianism 'should be resisted by all people who prize their individuality and independence of mind.'[12]

It is a strange irony indeed that it is now the Darwinists who stand accused of arrogance and authoritarianism. That was the same charge made, with considerable justification, against the church a century ago when Darwin's theory was first propounded. It is most noticeable that Darwinism has become virtually the sacred cow of modern science. It is normally in the nature of science to expose its theories to intellectual challenge. It is also increasingly the fashion for the work of scientists to be subjected to public scrutiny and debate. But not evolution! It is the protected species of science. No criticism can be tolerated. No alternative can be dispassionately considered. No other proposition can be accorded academic approval.

It is indeed a peculiar situation we have arrived at, particularly when the unavoidable truth is that science is very far from understanding how life originated. It is surely in everyone's interest to acknowledge that it is so. Of course, the moment we open our minds to the much more likely possibility that the origin of life is intricately associated with the existence and activity of a Creator, we go beyond scientific inquiry and into a realm where design, purpose and accountability rather than mechanistic or molecular considerations become the key issues. Perhaps it is because the study of origins has emotional and spiritual as well as intellectual dimensions that it has become an area where open debate is not readily tolerated.

Does anybody know for sure?

The desire to understand the origin of the world and of life itself is like no other activity that scientists and philosophers are involved in. The difference lies in that when you try to unravel what happened at the beginning of the universe you have to open your mind to the possibility that there are factors at work beyond the purely material and mechanistic. To rule out the existence of a Creator, in the face of so much evidence of intelligent design, is either an act of great faith or great folly! It is a bit like saying you are prepared to fully investigate the workings of a personal computer, but are not prepared to allow the existence of a programmer or technician. That is certainly not the approach of an objective and inquiring mind.

There is no doubt that the debate about Darwinism has been a source of discomfort and distress to many Christians. The almost universal acceptance of evolutionary and materialistic explanations of origins in western thought has often forced Christians who believe in a Creator into a somewhat beleaguered position. Of course, some believers have found comfort and occasionally excitement in sensing the possibility of harmonising the evolutionary and biblical positions, though it is noticeable that almost all the concessions have to be made by those who regard the Bible as God's word.

In light of the highly tentative and hugely speculative nature of much evolutionary thought, Christians should be much more confident in what they believe God has revealed about the origin of the world. Nor should they be afraid of open scientific inquiry into origins, for it is clear that God has made some of his purpose knowable through his works in nature.[13]

So what can we know? Well, if not all the details of creation, certainly the most important truths associated with it. These can be summarised as follows:

- God created the world out of nothing and he himself is distinct from it.[14]
- He created the world perfectly and progressively and entrusted it to us.[15]

- God sustains the world he has created and holds its history and its future in his hands.[16]
- Human beings are the pinnacle of his creation and reflect his own eternal being.[17]
- Human beings have defied the will of the Creator, become alienated from him and have fallen into sin.[18]
- Through the sacrifice of Jesus Christ, humans can find forgiveness and be restored to a right relationship with their Creator.[19]

We need to know!

I have worked in organisations where sensitive information was only passed on to others on a 'need to know' basis. Given the wealth of information we have from both theological revelation and scientific investigation about the nature of the world we inhabit, we can hardly claim that God has left us in the dark! It is surely obvious that God has entrusted to us as much as we need to know.

The Christian faith has an unashamedly dogmatic position about origins and their significance for the here and now. It was to a university audience at Athens two thousand years ago that St Paul declared: 'The God who made the world and everything in it is the LORD of heaven and earth ... but now he commands all people everywhere to repent. For he has set a day when he will judge the world with justice by the man (Jesus) he has appointed. He has given proof of this to all men by raising him from the dead.'[20]

For Christians, the bottom line is that our personal biography – how we live our lives – is just as important as the position we take about our personal biology – where we came from!

Notes

1   Stephen Jay Gould, *Wonderful Life*, p. 28.
2   Robert E.D. Clark, *Darwin, Before and After*, p. 88.
3   See, for example, Phillip E. Johnson, *Darwin on Trial*, chapter 4; Michael Denton, *Evolution, A Theory in Crisis*, chapter 8; Jonathan Wells, *Icons of Evolution*, chapters 4 and 10.
4   D.G. Mackean, *Life Study* p.191.
5   Quoted by Phillip E. Johnson in *Darwin on Trial*, p. 47.
6   Phillip E. Johnson, *Darwin on Trial*, p. 50.
7   F. Crick, *Life Itself*, p. 88.
8   F. Crick and L.E. Orgel, *Directed Panspermia*, 19:341-46.
9   M. Denton, *Evolution: A Theory in Crisis*, p. 271.
10 See for example D. Swift, *Evolution under the Microscope* (Leighton Academic Press, 2002).
11 M. Denton, *Evolution: A Theory in Crisis*, pp. 358-9.
12 R. Milton, *The Facts of Life*, pp. 297-8.
13 Bible, New Testament, Rom. 1:20.
14 Bible, Old Testament, Gen. 1:1.
15 Bible, Old Testament, Gen. 1:2-31.
16 Bible, New Testament, Col. 1:15-17; Heb. 1:1-3.
17 Bible, Old Testament, Gen. 1:26.
18 Bible, New Testament, Rom. 3:23.
19 Bible, New Testament, Rom. 5:1,2.
20 Bible, New Testament, Acts 17:24,30,31.

5

Reason or Naturalist Dogma?

Alastair Noble

Shortly after the Japanese attack on the American Fleet at Pearl Harbour in December 1941, the British Prime Minister, Winston Churchill, met with the Chief of the Imperial General Staff, General Alan Brooke, to assess the impact of this development on the war effort. The General complained that the attack had undone many days of work by his staff in trying to anticipate an assault against British interests in the Pacific. Churchill's response was simply, 'So, we've won the war after all!' What he saw was that the entry of America into the war, despite the awful tragedy in Hawaii, removed any doubt about the eventual outcome of the conflict. In his biography of Churchill, Roy Jenkins comments that the incident showed the difference in outlook of a fine staff officer and a world statesman.[1]

It all depends on how you look at it, we often say to one another in discussion. What we usually mean is that we don't agree with what is being said and we take a different view. The truth is that few of us approach any situation with complete objectivity. Our bias may come from our social or educational background. Sometimes a bad experience colours our judgement or, equally, a significant success gives a new perspective. To recognise that our outlook is, in substantial measure, determined by our previous experiences is to begin to understand why we think as we do.

It is not surprising, therefore, that our most fundamental beliefs are conditioned by our formative experiences. In fact, each of us, whether we realise it or not, has a basic world-view which largely determines how we think and how we live our lives. Religious and philosophical ideas play a much greater part in our thinking than we would at first concede.

Surveying religious belief

Our planet is a deeply religious place. If you are surprised by this, consider the following data on the religious beliefs of the people of our world[2]

- Christianity   33%
- Islam   20%
- Hinduism   13%
- Chinese folk religion   6%
- Buddhism   6%
- Ethnic religions   4%
- Atheism   3%
- All other religions (9) 2%
- *No religion*   13%

What is striking, apart from the prime position of Christianity in world terms, is that only 13 per cent of the world's population claim to have no religion and only 3 per cent assert that they are atheists. Although the religious convictions of the others will range from the 'only nominal' to the 'very committed', you still can't escape the conclusion that humans are essentially religious beings. Even among those who profess not to be at all religious, the widespread use of horoscopes and fortune-telling betrays a residual sense of the supernatural.

In the increasingly secular West, these figures may come as something of a surprise. But the position in Britain is no less intriguing, as the National Census of 2001 showed. This was the first time the population of the United Kingdom was asked about personal religious beliefs and what emerged is astonishing. The religious loyalties of the British are[3]

- Christianity   72%
- Islam   3%
- Hinduism   1%
- All other religions   2%
- *No religion*   15%
- *Not stated*   7%

You would have to say it was certainly worth asking the question! Otherwise we probably would not have guessed that more than 70 per cent of Britons consider themselves to be Christians in a general sense or that only 15 per cent (23 per cent if you include those who did not respond) have no religious faith. So much for frequent assertion that Britain is no longer a Christian country!

Taking a world-view

When you look more closely at the various faith or no-faith positions, you come to the conclusion that there are essentially only three world-views. These basic beliefs can be simply summarised as

- Theism – there is a God.
- Atheism – there is no God.
- Pantheism – everything is God.

It could be argued that agnosticism should be added to this list, although it is debatable whether it is a separate world-view. It really describes an inability to decide which world-view is valid, though, in fairness, some agnostics hold the firm view that it is impossible to know whether there is a God or not. For all practical purposes, therefore, agnosticism as a world-view is similar to atheism.

Theism

One dictionary defines theism as 'belief in one God as the transcendent creator and ruler of the universe that does not necessarily entail further belief in divine revelation'. It is, by far, the dominant world-view, but that, clearly, does not imply that there is a shared understanding of the nature of God and of what he has revealed to us. The key word, though, is 'transcendent', indicating that God's existence is of a different order from the natural world of which we are part.

Theism is not just widespread – a significant phenomenon in itself – but it is also intellectually satisfying. Our planet teems with life of every conceivable form. It is home to highly sophisticated human beings. It lies within a hugely complex and dynamic universe. All this demands an explanation for its existence that goes much further than vague suggestions about chance and accident. And not only the physical world, but something deeply emotional within us cries out for some answer that indicates we are here because an Intelligent Designer planned it that way.

The sceptic will immediately object that to accept the existence of a Creator is only to postpone the ultimate question. Put simply, where did the Creator come from? But to ask that question is to miss the point. Theistic belief is the acceptance of the transcendent and that there is, beyond the world of time and space which we inhabit, existence of a different and timeless kind. In such a sphere, the theist believes, God exists.

And such a belief is not so fantastic. Part of the theory of relativity as developed by Einstein suggests that if we were able to travel at the speed of light, time would stand still. That doesn't sound very different from saying that there is another kind of existence where time becomes irrelevant. We certainly find it difficult to think of time other than as a linear phenomenon, with past, present and future. But what if there is a realm where there is no time, or in which the past and future coexist in an eternal present? That sounds remarkably like what Moses, the great leader of the monotheistic Jewish nation, expressed more than three thousand years ago: 'Before the mountains were born or you brought forth the earth and the world, from everlasting to everlasting you are God.'[4] Perhaps, too, Einstein glimpsed this when he expressed the view that the mathematical precision of the universe reveals the mathematical mind of God.

If you accept the existence of God and his active participation in the creation of the world as a self-evident truth, it changes drastically the nature of the inquiry into origins. The intricacies and inconsistencies of the debate about the role of big bangs, black holes, amino acids, primeval soups, RNA and DNA, genes, cells, mutations and fossils become fairly secondary considerations. It is not that they are unimportant by any means, but no longer central to the puzzle. When an Intelligent Designer is perceived to be at the heart of the universe, the rest of the detail is manageable, or even peripheral to the central truths of our existence!

Atheism

Atheism, by contrast, is the straightforward rejection of any belief in God. It leaves no room for negotiation. To the atheist, God simply does not exist. For better or for worse, the natural world is all there is.

If this belief – and belief it is – is the easiest to describe, it is surely the hardest to defend. In many ways, atheism requires a huge measure of faith in one's judgement and it begs the question as to how can anyone know for sure that there is nothing beyond the material world, especially when all the evidence points in the opposite direction. Perhaps this is why, in terms of popular acceptance, it trails well behind most major faith positions. But the influence of atheism on the world should never be underestimated. The huge communist empires of the modern world, with their official state atheism, and their satellite countries show how the dogma of a tiny minority can be imposed on vast populations. That many of these systems are now being dismantled is small comfort to the millions of people whose lives were blighted by their totalitarian arrogance.

The few atheists I have met have not always been consistent about their belief. While they will readily reject the idea of God, they often have not thought through the alternative. If God does not exist, then what else must have been there before the universe as we know it? Matter? Energy? Black holes? Quantum mechanics? Creative possibility? There must have been something! Even blind chance needs something to work on! The widespread idea that the universe just exists and we better just accept it is more of an evasion than an explanation!

My experience also is that some people become atheists because they have been repelled from faith by the occasional arrogance of religious groups or individuals and their unwillingness to engage in serious debate. But that's a poor reason for turning away from the compelling evidences of the Creator's existence. It may be understandable, but it doesn't make atheism any more secure.

Atheism will always take the view that, since there is no God, the universe must somehow be self-generating. Despite what many would consider to be a blindingly obvious flaw in that assumption, atheistic thought will always try to find support for its position in scientific observations. No matter how slight the evidence or tenuous the connections, the basic conclusion will always be the same. Somehow it is imagined that if you understand a part of the process by which things happen, you can dispose of the idea that a Greater Mind devised it in the first place. It is a bit like saying that if you understand how a part of a motor car works you have removed the need to believe in a manufacturer. Such is the power of a worldview that such illogicalities can be accepted without question in the most distinguished centres of higher education! St Paul encountered the same kind of thinking in his time and concluded, most controversially, that its proponents, 'although they claimed to be wise, ... became fools'.[5]

Atheism is a bleak and ultimately destructive view. No God. No purpose. No future. And no particular reason for upholding moral principles. Why does anything matter in the end other than self-preservation? It's not at all surprising that soldiers claimed there were no atheists in the trenches. Confronted with the crises of life, atheism provides no sanctuary and no comfort. Unless, of course, passing into oblivion is a steadying influence. But then, what if atheism got it wrong?

Pantheism

Pantheism is a more diffuse belief system which is at the heart of a number of Eastern religions including Buddhism and Hinduism. It is built around the doctrine that

God is the transcendent reality of which humankind, nature and the material universe are manifestations. In some forms, it regards God as identical with the material universe and the forces of nature. In other forms, it accepts the existence of a number of gods.

Certainly, pantheism acknowledges the great mystery of existence and attempts to rationalise it, either by proposing a host of deities or by incorporating all of life into the nature of God. It is, in some ways, almost a halfway house between believing in no god and a single, personal God. However, pantheism is highly speculative, lacks clarity, fails to distinguish between temporal and eternal phenomena and creates an illusion of harmony where none exists, as in the case of a rationalisation of suffering as the product of unworthy desire. It also removes any sense that God is personal and knowable.

In biblical times, pantheism in its various pagan and philosophical forms was a huge challenge both to Jewish monotheism – belief in only one true God – and Christian theism – belief in the one true God who revealed himself to the world in Jesus Christ. In our time, pantheism is much less of a challenge as the debate in the increasingly secular west has largely shifted to whether there is any God or none!

In its historic forms, pantheism introduced a huge element of unpredictability into an understanding of the world. If there are many gods and they are occasionally in conflict with each other, the world becomes a highly uncertain and capricious place. In its more modern forms, it has become a more mystical and indefinite philosophy, capable of accommodating most personal spiritual aspirations and advocating environmentally-friendly and calmer lifestyles. Some expressions of pantheism teach reincarnation and endless regeneration, but do not immediately commend themselves as having the definitive

answer on origins. Indeed, they only push back the ultimate questions!

Agnosticism

It is worth considering the position of the agnostic, since
many people who claim to have no religious faith would
stop short of saying they are full-blown atheists. Some say
they just don't know whether there is a God or not while
others claim that it is not possible to know about a
Supreme Being or Ultimate Cause. Only natural phenomena, they assert, can be known.

Whereas atheists deny the existence of God, agnostics
raise a different question about the 'knowability' of God.
The thoughtful agnostic has understood the limits of
rationality in explaining the origin of the universe and its
inability to make much headway in understanding the
nature of a Creator. But the proposition that we can never
know about the Creator is spurious. Just as we could only
know what goes on in government offices behind the Official Secrets Act when someone leaks information, so it
would be possible to know about God if he chooses to
reveal himself. And that kind of revelation demands, as
we saw in Chapter 1, the response of faith.

Agnosticism may not be inclined to accept religious
interpretations of reality, but it should at least accept the
possibility that, if God does exist, he would almost certainly wish to make himself known.

Naturally dogmatic!

On the whole, we are conditioned to believe that while
Christians, football supporters and politicians are

hopelessly biased, intellectuals, academics and the politi-
cally-correct groups are capable only of wholly objective
and dispassionate thinking! Nothing could be further
from the truth. If we are really honest, we would admit
that all our thinking is, to some extent, conditioned by the
world-view we hold to.

It is certainly the case that each of us has arrived at a
particular world-view for a variety of reasons – some
intellectual, some social, some emotional. It is also possible that we may change our world view in the light of
experience. But what is unlikely to be the case is that we
arrive at conclusions about the fundamental questions of
our existence in isolation from the general views we hold
about life.

When Richard Dawkins, the great advocate of evolutionary science, defines biology as 'the study of complicated things that give the appearance of having been
designed for a purpose' you begin to suspect that an atheistic presupposition is overriding a more obvious theistic
conclusion. And when he writes, 'I want to persuade the
reader, not just that the Darwinian world-view *happens* to
be true, but that it is the only known theory that *could*, in
principle, solve the mystery of our existence', it is clear
that the basis of his position is a philosophical one – or to
use his actual phrase – 'a world-view', and an atheistic one
at that.[6]

Indeed, Dawkins' idea of a 'blind watchmaker', as
opposed to the older creationist analogy of the intelligent
watchmaker, is just the kind of memorable but meaningless proposition we have become conditioned to accept
without question. Phillip Johnson, a distinguished lawyer
and academic who has made a careful study of the evidence for evolution,[7] insists that Dawkins does visually-
handicapped people a great disservice with his use of this
idea. Such people, he argues, often have heightened

abilities in other directions and are capable of the most remarkable feats – consider, for instance, the progress of David Blunkett to a political career at the highest level. Dawkins' watchmaker, Johnson insists, would have to be not just blind, but comatose as well!

It is a peculiar irony that an analogy Dawkins uses in *The Blind Watchmaker* to illustrate the compelling nature of Darwinian evolution is a simple experiment he performed on his computer.[8] The variety of patterns his basic program generated helped him to understand the potential of evolution for producing a wide range of life forms. The analogy seems to miss completely the point that without a programmer's mind to write the first program, none of it would have happened. It provides a much better illustration of theistic creation than atheistic evolution!

Dr Michael Ruse, a well-known Canadian philosopher of science, came much closer to admitting the real status of evolutionary theory. At a symposium entitled 'the New Antievolutionism' at the American Association for the Advancement of Science in 1993 he virtually admitted that evolution is based on a dogmatic exclusion of a supernatural creation or Creator. 'At some very basic level,' he said, 'evolution as a scientific theory makes a commitment to a kind of naturalism, namely that at some level one is going to exclude miracles and these sorts of things, come what may.' He continued, 'Evolution, akin to religion, involves making certain a priori or metaphysical assumptions, which at some level cannot be proven empirically.'[9] Well, at least that is honest and we know where we stand.

Evolution, as understood by Ruse, is actually a philosophy, not a science, and is in effect a belief system or worldview. But on another occasion and in a much more sinister vein Ruse claimed: 'I realise that when one is dealing with people, say, at school level, or these sorts of things, certain sorts of arguments are appropriate. But those of us who are academics ... should recognise ... that the science side has certain metaphysical assumptions built into doing science, which – it may not be a good thing to admit in a court of law – but I think that in honesty that we should recognise, and that we should be thinking about some of these sorts of things.'[10] If I understand that properly, I think it means that our honesty about what we believe should be selective in terms of the audiences with whom we should share it.

What all this really demonstrates is that we are mentally conditioned to work from assumptions to conclusions. Much evolutionary thought, it seems, starts from the assumption that there cannot be a Creator. A different view starts from the assumption that there is a Creator and that he is the initiator of the universe as we know it. Philosophical or religious assumptions, or world-views, may be right or wrong, but it seems they are unavoidable!

Christian theism

Theism starts from the position that the universe is constructed the way it is because God made it so. To theists this is a self-evident fact. Voltaire once expressed a view that all theists share: 'I shall always be convinced that a watch proves a watchmaker and that a universe proves a God.'

And theism is, in every sense, a liberating position. The starting point of a Creator makes sense of the universe and gives an ultimate reference point for what we may discover about the natural world in other ways. We don't need to agonise over how the universe started or how life emerged. These events occurred as a direct result of the Creator's actions. If we uncover through scientific investigations or by other means some clues as to the processes by which the world operates, so much the better. Biochemical or geological puzzles may or may not, in the end, be solved. Our understanding is always likely to be incomplete but, to the theist, the basic conclusion about the existence of the Creator is never in doubt.

However, a purely theistic view does not tell us very much about what God is like. Christian theism takes our understanding a great deal further, believing that God has revealed to us in his Son Jesus Christ that he is personal and loving. That is of course a theological angle, but no less valid than other insights into God's existence and nature.

Some years ago, I got lost when I was driving through Belfast. I stopped at a petrol station to ask for directions, and was given that most helpful of advice. 'If I was trying to get to there, I wouldn't start from here!' In thinking about the most fundamental aspects of our existence, we have to start from where we are. But there is absolutely no reason why we should not arrive at where we ought to be! For many, only Christian revelation takes them there.

Notes

1   R. Jenkins, *Churchill* (Macmillan, 2001).
2   Source – *Encyclopaedia Britannica*, 2003.
3   National Census, 2001, on www.statistics.gov.uk.
4   Bible, Old Testament, Ps. 90:2.
5   Bible, New Testament, Rom. 1:21-23.
6   R. Dawkins, *The Blind Watchmaker*, p. 1 and preface p. xiv.
7   See for example, P. Johnson, *Darwin on Trial*, and *Wedge of Truth*.
8   R. Dawkins, *The Blind Watchmaker*, chapter 3.
9   A transcript of the talk is available from the National Centre for Science Education, PO Box 9477, Berkeley, CA 94709-0477, USA. It is also quoted in www.answersingenesis.org/doc/1342.
10 Also quoted in www.answersingenesis.org/doc/1342.

6

Reading is believing!

Stephen McQuoid

Christianity has often been described as a religion of the book. This is a fair description as Christians get their doctrines and ethics from the Bible. It goes without saying, therefore, that the credibility of the Bible is of utmost importance. But how can we be sure that the Bible is a reliable book? How do we really know that it is the word of God? In this and the next two chapters I will deal with these questions.

An inspired work

Why should the Bible be considered to be the word of God? In answering this question we need to firstly note that the Bible itself claims to be the word of God. This, of course, is not necessarily proof that it is what it claims to be, but it is an important point to make because it is the obvious starting point in the defence of the Bible. The Bible's own understanding of itself brings us to the point where this claim needs to be investigated.

The Bible's claim to be the word of God is one which is repeated on numerous occasions. Indeed on some 394 occasions in the Old Testament the phrase, 'the word of

God' is used. The New Testament also refers to the Old Testament, many times, as the 'word of God'. It is also important to note the precise language which the Bible employs as it describes itself.

In 2 Timothy 3:16 we read, 'All scripture is inspired' (NRSV).[1] The word inspired is used very loosely in modern speech. I am a big football fan and when watching football on television I have often heard the commentator say, 'That was an inspired piece of play.' The word has also been used to refer to the work of a great composer, or even a brilliant move made by a military general. When the Bible uses the term 'inspired' of itself, it means that God through his Holy Spirit was involved in the writing process. What we have on the page are not just the thoughts of some human author, but of God himself. As Peter states '… prophecy never had its origin in the will of man, but men spoke from God as they were carried along by the Holy Spirit' (2 Pet.1:21). Of course, the individual writers put their own distinctive style into their writings, and therefore the penning of Scripture was not just some form of mechanical dictation. Nevertheless, the Bible claims that its origin is in the very mind of God.

Jesus' view of Scripture

But as well as the Bible itself claiming that it is divinely inspired, Jesus also saw it as the word of God. Probably the most powerful argument in favour of the Bible being the word of God is the testimony of Jesus on the matter. Jesus unequivocally put his full seal of approval on the Old Testament (Mt. 5:18) and he continually quoted the Old Testament, applying it to situations that he found himself in. He also stated that his followers would receive divine help so that they could pass on what they saw and heard for successive generations (Jn. 14:26). The recommendations of Jesus, as well as the comments made by the New Testament writers, clearly demonstrate the divine nature of the Bible. If Jesus is God, and there is ample evidence to substantiate that claim,[2] and if he declared the Bible to be the word of God, then it must be accepted as such.

A remarkable coherence

In addition to the Bible's claims about itself, and Jesus' commendation of it, we need to note that when the Bible is seen as a whole, it is remarkably coherent. This is astonishing bearing in mind that the Bible was written by more than forty authors from vastly different backgrounds and cultural perspectives, and it was written over a period of twelve hundred years. That being the case, one would expect the Bible to be a collection of fairly random ideas forced together in an artificial way. However, what we do observe is that there is a single thread throughout, and that thread is God's plan of salvation for humanity. It is proclaimed consistently and anyone who is familiar with the Bible will marvel at its unity and absence of contradiction. The reason for this is clear: although there were many authors, there was only one source, God himself.

The confirmation of history and archaeology

Although the Bible is a book full of spiritual truths, it is also grounded in history. It was written within human culture and tells the story of God's people and how they related to him within the wider context of human history. This can be verified by historians and archaeologists.

The historical reliability of the Bible is accepted by many in the world of academia. Some of the biblical writers deliberately included historical references so that we would know the historic nature of the events they were recording. In Luke 3:1, for example, Luke includes numerous historical references in just a few lines. For example he mentions the rule of Tiberius Caesar and the governorship of Pontius Pilate. There is also mention of Herod of Galilee and his brother Philip as well as Lysanias the Tetrarch. Each of these people can be cross-referenced with what we know of the history of the period, and this will demonstrate the Bible's reliability. It is also interesting to compare the Bible with other historical works of the time. The Jewish historian Josephus, for example, mentions numerous figures that are introduced to us in the Bible, and in so doing provides confirmation of the Bible's historicity.

But as well as being historically credible, the Bible is also supported by archaeology. The science of archaeology does two things in relation to the Bible. Firstly, it confirms the accuracy of the biblical accounts, and secondly, it provides greater insight into the biblical text. As we have already noted, the Bible makes numerous references to historical places, people and events. It also notes geographical features and cultural norms. Through archaeology we can confirm these with hard evidence.

Interestingly, archaeology has also overturned a number of theories which questioned the reliability of the Bible. In the nineteenth century it was a common practice amongst many scholars to treat the Bible as a book of myths and legends. Some claimed that Abraham was a fictitious figure along with the Hittite peoples. They also claimed that Moses could not have written the introductory books of the Bible because writing had not been invented in his day. Questions were asked about the historical reliability of the book of Acts. Since then archaeology has refuted these claims to the point where it would be hard to find a serious scholar who would still concur with the findings of their nineteenth-century counterparts. Indeed Jewish archaeologist Nelson Glueck states that, 'no archaeological discovery has ever been made that contradicts or even controverts historical statements in scripture'.[3] This historical and archaeological support of the biblical text adds credence to its claim to be the word of God.

An undeniable power

Another reason for believing the Bible to be the word of God is its transformative power. There is an old expression that says, 'The proof of the pudding is in the eating.' It refers to the fact that even when we are presented with a theoretical proposition, it is often not enough to convince us to believe. What we need is to see that this proposition works in real life.

It so happens that there is ample evidence of the power of the Bible. Countless millions of people have been transformed and have experienced a completely new lifestyle through reading and believing the Bible. People in many countries and cultures have gone through dramatic transformations when they opened themselves up to the Bible's power. It could also be argued that evangelists like Dr Billy Graham have been enormously influential on a global scale, primarily because they base their message on the teachings of the Bible.

Objectors might also argue that such evidence for the Bible's power can be put down to subjective emotionalism and not empirical science. This may be the case, though subjective or not the evidence of the Bible's transformative power throughout history is undeniable.

Those who do object to the idea that the Bible is the word of God still have to find a satisfactory explanation as to why the Bible, like no other book, has impacted the history of human existence, along with our current civilisation, and continues to do so.

The reality of prophecy

A final reason for believing that the Bible is the word of God is the presence and fulfilment of prophecy within the Bible. This evidence is remarkable and compelling, and can be put to the test. Biblical prophecy is a distinctive and common genre within the Bible, and a very important one. The Bible itself makes it clear that fulfilled prophecy is evidence of the divine origin of the Bible (Jer. 28:9; Deut. 18:21,22). It is to this evidence that we will turn in the next chapter.

What about other holy works?

Before we do so, however, an important question must be raised. Even if we accept that the Bible is the word of God, what about other religious books that make the same claim? For many people the Bible is just another religious book, no different from the Koran or the *Bhagavada Gita*. Why do Christians believe that the Bible is the word of God in a particular and exclusive way?

In answering this question we need to think about the philosophical issue of what is true and what is not true. In our post-modern society there is no such thing as absolute truth. Everyone has their own truth and no one truth can claim supremacy over another. In relation to the Bible, therefore, it should only be seen as the truth held by one particular religious community. Our post-modern culture does not permit the Bible to be the only truth.

This way of looking at things may appear convenient, but there is a problem. What happens when two truth claims prove to be mutually contradictory? For example, some have claimed that Christians, Muslims and Hindus all worship the same God. But when you look at how the respective scriptures of these world religions describe the nature and character of God, the various accounts contradict each other. For the Christian, God exits within a trinity, for the Muslim, God is one, and for the Hindu, there are many gods. Such contradictory views cannot all be right. To claim that they are is to fly in the face of logic.

It may be culturally acceptable to say that they are all shades of the same truth, but in reality such a position is nonsense. It would be as illogical as suggesting that red and blue are actually the same colour. It may be politically correct, but it is foolish, and when we are dealing with an issue as important as our eternal destiny then the stakes are too high to risk all for the sake of political correctness. So what are we to make of the Bible and other scriptures?

Ultimately a decision has to be made as to which of the many religious scriptures we accept as being the truth. The Bible, however, has already made its case. It has an excellent pedigree and good reason to be accepted as the truth. It is against this yardstick that all other religious works must be compared. When all is said and done, any book which claims to be the word of God must have the same credibility attached to its claims as the Bible does. It is not enough that another scripture appears to be good, helpful, or even revered by many. Any rival work must clearly demonstrate clear justification for its claim to be the word of God.

It must have the endorsement of a unique individual who himself has excellent credentials.[4] It must be able to demonstrate an exceptional quality such as containing numerous prophesies that are then fulfilled, and it must be consistent throughout. In addition, it must have a transformative power that can not only affect the individual, but entire civilisations, and it must be confirmed by historical and archaeological evidence. Any rival work that does not match up to this list of criteria fails, for the Bible has achieved this list in every part.

Once you have the standard work, there is no need for lesser ones. The Bible is unique among the world's religious scriptures. It deserves to be accepted as the word of God, a position which automatically denies recognition to any other religious work.

Notes

1 Some translations use the words 'God-breathed'.
2 The evidence for the deity of Christ will be dealt with in a later chapter.
3 Nelson Glueck, in *Christianity for Sceptics* by Steve Kumar, p.110.
4 The credentials that Jesus possesses are dealt with in chapter 10. The most impressive of his credentials is that he rose from the dead, something which no other founder of a world religion has achieved.

7

Back to the future

Stephen McQuoid

One of the primary reasons for believing in the unique-ness of the Bible is the presence of biblical prophecy. As we approach the subject of biblical prophecy, we need firstly to deal with some important definitions. Within the general genre of biblical prophetic literature, there are two kinds of prophecy. These are sometimes referred to as 'foretelling' and 'forth-telling'. In the latter the prophet was giving God's commentary on a situation that was going on at that time. He was, in a sense, God's mouth-piece telling people how they should behave. The former of these was prophecy that contained a predictive ele-ment. The prophet would make a prediction that would come true at a later point in history, often very much later. It is this category which provides compelling evidence for the belief that the Bible is the word of God.

When it comes to this predictive prophecy, we can iden-tify three kinds in the Old Testament. Firstly, there are pre-dictions about the coming of the Messiah. For the sake of convenience I will label these as 'Messianic prophecies'. Secondly, there are predictions about kings, nations and cities. I will refer to these as 'historical prophecies'. Thirdly, there are predictions about the future of the Jews. I will refer to these as 'national Israel prophecies'. We will focus particularly on the first two categories. That is, prophecies about historical events, and prophecies about the coming of the Messiah.

Before we do this, however, some things need to be said about prophecy in general. Sceptics might argue that prophecy is not adequate evidence for the inspiration of the Bible because there have been many non-biblical prophets in history who have made predictions. That being the case there is no reason to see biblical prophecy as being anything special. Of course, that there have been other prophets in human history is a point that I would readily concede. Some, like Nostradamus, were secular prophets, while others like Charles Taze Russell were religious prophets. But the mere presence of prophets outside of the Bible is not, in itself, sufficient evidence to deny the uniqueness of biblical prophecy. After all, the point is not whether other people made prophecies, but rather, whether or not the prophecies made by others were of the same calibre as the prophecies found in the Bible.

The burden of proof on this issue rests with the sceptic. He has to make his case, because, as I will demonstrate in this chapter, the prophecies in the Bible are staggering in their quality. If other prophecies are to be taken as seriously as those found in the Bible, then they need to be demonstrably of the same quality as biblical prophecies. But if they cannot be demonstrated to be of the same quality, then it must be conceded by every reasonable person, that both biblical prophecy, and the Bible itself, are unique. More than that, it would be proof that the Bible is indeed the word of God.

The most convenient way of assessing the credibility of a prophecy, including biblical prophecies, is to set up a series of benchmarks, or standards, to which these prophecies have to adhere. Only in this way can any sort of quality control be achieved, and the credibility of a particular prophecy be established. When benchmarks are used, it is interesting to note that prophecies outside of the Bible do rather poorly, whereas biblical prophecies do very well. There are three benchmarks that prove useful in this regard.

The benchmark of predictability

The first benchmark that should be used is that of predictability. This benchmark tests a prophecy by asking if the fulfilment of the prophecy is in some way surprising, or merely predictable. For example, supposing I was to make the following prophecy: *There will be a conflict between a major democracy and a totalitarian regime over the next one hundred years.* Any casual observer would think it rather *passé*. You certainly would not celebrate and hail me as the greatest genius who ever lived. The reason is that we would be expecting something like this to happen anyway. Indeed a person with no 'gift' for prophecy would easily be able to make such a prediction. Of course, predictability does not in itself invalidate a prophecy. My prophecy, though bland, could still have been genuine. But it would be utterly unimpressive, and when fulfilled, it would not be of sufficient calibre to convince anyone of my prophetic abilities.

A great many of the non-biblical prophecies fall into this category. Indeed more often than not when non-biblical prophets have made their predictions, the predictions were so unsurprising that they were utterly unimpressive. Therefore our attitude to them can reasonably be summed up in the words, 'so what!' In reality they prove nothing.

The benchmark of ambiguity

A second benchmark that can be used to test the mettle of a prophecy is that of ambiguity. In this test a prophecy is investigated to see if what it predicts is specific or general. Clearly a specific prophecy, if fulfilled, would carry considerably more weight.

For example, supposing I were to make this prophecy: *A great power will be humbled and a great wealth lost*. If no further details were given, you could take this prophecy to refer to several things. It could be interpreted as a reference to economic problems in several wealthy countries such as America, Japan, Germany, or even the United Kingdom. Equally you could interpret this prophecy to refer to a political organisation such as the European Union or the United Nations. You might see it as a reference to a powerful multinational such as ICI, BP or Enron. Conceivably you could even interpret this prophecy as referring to a powerful individual such as Bill Gates, Richard Branson or George Soros. The point is that the prediction would be so ambiguous in nature that its meaning could be stretched to include almost any difficulty that was experienced by any of the above. If the USA went into recession, if the EU ran into trouble with its expansion, if a multinational went bust or if Bill Gates lost an antitrust law suite, then I could claim that the prophecy had been fulfilled. But with such flexibility of interpretation, a supposed fulfilment would be so unspectacular, it would become meaningless as a prophecy.

Again many of the non-biblical prophecies have been so ambiguous, they could fit into several situations. For this reason they too are unimpressive. Once again they fall far short of the benchmarks and cannot therefore be given too much respect.

The benchmark of accurate fulfilment

The third benchmark that should be applied to any prophecy is that of whether or not it has actually been fulfilled. It stands to reason that if I prophecy something and it does not happen, then my ability as a prophet should be called into question. No one would be able to take me seriously as a prophet, because there would be no empirical evidence that I had any ability to make prophecies.

Here too many of history's prophets have failed dismally. Their predictions have simply proved to be downright wrong. For example, prophecies made by the writers of *The Watchtower* magazine which was founded by 'prophet' Charles Taze Russell, have often proved faulty. Russell himself made several questionable prophecies, and this trend was then followed by his successor Joseph Franklin Rutherford. On one occasion Rutherford prophesied that 1925 would see the, 'completion of all things'.[1] At this time, he stated, there would be a universal war in which all people who were not Jehovah's Witnesses would be destroyed. Those who were Jehovah's Witnesses would be spared to live in a heavenly and an earthly paradise.

So convinced were many of his followers that they gave up their jobs and sold their homes in expectation. But like many other non-biblical prophecies, this simply did not come about. Likewise the great secular prophet Nostradamus had a very poor success rate in the fulfilment of his prophecies, as well as being guilty of failing the first two benchmarks. It is impossible to see any connection between the majority of his prophecies and any known event which has actually occurred. The result is that his as well as the prophecies of many others are ultimately unconvincing.

Interestingly, a survey was carried out between 1975 and 1981 of some noted psychics to see if their prophecies would prove accurate.[2] In total 72 predictions were made with only six of them being fulfilled in any way. That meant that 66 of the predictions proved to be downright wrong. Of the six that were in some way correct, two were ambiguous and two were unsurprising. They therefore failed the ambiguity and predictability tests. This rate of fulfilment can only be described as pathetic. But this is not unusual. Indeed there is no evidence outside of the Bible that any prophet has proved to be consistently correct.

Having stated what the benchmarks should be, they must then be applied to the prophecies mentioned in the Bible, to see if they contain any degree of credibility. When this is done, Biblical prophecies, in contrast to all others, are very impressive indeed. When all the benchmarks are applied and biblical prophecies are put to the test, they pass with flying colours.

Predictability

Firstly, far from being expected, the kind of prophecies that we read about in the Bible are surprising and unexpected. For example the prophecies about the Messiah suffering would have puzzled many Jews who were expecting history to be consummated by a military Messiah who would rid his people of the yoke of oppression. So when Jesus came as Messiah, and when he was crucified in fulfilment of these prophecies, even his disciples were taken by surprise and were stunned by what had happened.

Ambiguity

Secondly, biblical prophecies have a tendency to be specific as opposed to being vague. So specific indeed that the Messianic prophecies predicted the very place of Jesus' birth, the fact that he would be born of a virgin and the fact that he would die a terrible and cruel death. Of particular interest are the passages that describe the death of Jesus. The description given is consistent with the Roman method of crucifixion, and yet at the time the predictions were made, this method of crucifixion had yet to be invented. More remarkable still is the fact that Jesus' bones were not broken during his crucifixion, just as had been prophesied. This is remarkable because the breaking of a prisoner's legs was very much part of the routine of crucifixion.

Fulfilment

Thirdly, all the biblical prophecies that have been fulfilled to date have been fulfilled accurately and completely. Though some of the prophecies in the Bible are yet to be fulfilled, this is because they refer to events which are still future. But the prophecies that were meant to be fulfilled, like for example the Messianic prophecies, have been, and in every detail.

To illustrate this point, we will now look at some examples of these fulfilled prophecies and note just how remarkable their fulfilment really is. Firstly, we will look at an example of the fulfilment of an historical prophecy, and secondly we will look at numerous examples of fulfilled Messianic prophecies.

The Old Testament prophet Ezekiel made a bold prediction that the city of Tyre would be destroyed. It was bold because at the time this prophecy was made, Tyre was a thriving city and one which did not feel threatened by its enemies. Not only did Ezekiel prophesy Tyre's destruction, he also predicted that the city would never be restored.

Remarkably this historic prophecy was fulfilled. Firstly Tyre was attacked by Nebuchadnezzar in his bid to become the world's great power. Then Alexander the Great attacked the city, leaving it in ruins. These two unrelated invasions demonstrate the remarkable accuracy of this Old Testament prophecy.

Having noted the above example, we will now look at the fulfilment of Messianic prophecies. For the purposes of emphasis, we will look at not just one Messianic prophecy, but a whole list. But it is important to realise that this list is not exhaustive; indeed there are at least sixty-one Messianic prophecies, all of which Jesus fulfilled.[3] The following chart compares the original prophecy with its Messianic fulfilment.

(All Bible quotes below from New American Standard Version)

Prophecy: Therefore the LORD himself will give you a sign: Behold, the virgin shall conceive a son. (Is. 7:14)

Fulfilment: She was found with child of the Holy Spirit ... Joseph ... did not know her till she had brought forth her firstborn. (Mt. 1:18,25)

Prophecy: There shall come forth a Rod from the stem of Jesse. (Is. 11:1)

Fulfilment: Jesus ... the son of Jesse (Lk. 3:23,32)

Prophecy: But you, Bethlehem Ephrathah, though you are little among the thousands of Judah, Yet out of you will come forth to me the one to be ruler over Israel. (Mich. 5:2)

Fulfilment: Jesus was born in Bethlehem of Judea. (Mt. 2:1)

Prophecy: The kings of Tarshish and of the isles will bring presents; the kings of Sheba and Seba will offer gifts. (Ps. 72:10)

Fulfilment: Wise men from the East came ... and they opened their treasures and presented their gifts to him. (Mt. 2:1,11)

Prophecy: A voice was heard in Ramah, Lamentation and bitter weeping, Rachel weeping for her children, refusing to be comforted for her children. Because they are no more. (Jer. 31:15)

Fulfilment: Then Herod, when he saw that he was deceived by the wise men, was exceedingly angry ... put to death all male children who were in Bethlehem. (Mt. 2:16)

Prophecy: Because zeal for your house has eaten me up, and the reproaches of those who reproach you have fallen on me. (Ps. 69:9)

Fulfilment: He made a whip of cords and drove them all out of the temple. (Jn. 2:15)

Prophecy: Then the eyes of the blind will be opened, and the ears of the deaf will be unstopped. Then the lame will leap like a deer, and the tongue of the dumb will sing for joy. (Is. 35:5,6)

Fulfilment: And Jesus was going about all the cities and villages ... healing every kind of disease and every kind of sickness. (Mt. 9:35)

Prophecy: Behold your king is coming to you ... lowly and riding on a donkey, a colt, the foal of a donkey. (Zech. 9:9)

Fulfilment: And they brought him to Jesus. And they threw their own clothes on the colt, and they set Jesus on him. (Lk. 19:35)

Prophecy: Even my familiar friend in whom I trusted, who ate my bread, has lifted up his heel against me. (Ps. 41:9)

Fulfilment: Judas Iscariot, who also betrayed him. (Mt. 10:4)

Prophecy: So they weighed out for my wages thirty pieces of silver. (Zech. 11:12)

Fulfilment: And they counted out to him thirty pieces of silver. (Mt. 26:15)

Prophecy: So I took the thirty pieces of silver and threw them into the house of the LORD for the potter. (Zech.11:13)

Fulfilment: Then he threw down the pieces of silver in the temple and departed ... And they consulted together and bought with them the potter's field, to bury strangers in. (Mt. 27:5– 7)

Prophecy: I gave my back to those who struck me, and my cheeks to those who plucked out the beard; I did not hide my face from shame and spitting. (Is. 50:6)

Fulfilment: Then they spat in his face and beat him; and others struck him with the palms of their hands. (Mt. 26:67)

Prophecy: They pierced my hands and my feet. (Ps. 22:16)

Fulfilment: And when they came to the place called Calvary, they crucified him. (Lk. 23:33)

Prophecy: They divided my garments among them, and for my clothing they cast lots. (Ps. 22:18)

Fulfilment: The soldiers, when they had crucified Jesus, took his garments ... They said 'Let us not tear it, but cast lots for it'. (Jn. 19:23, 24)

Prophecy: They gave me gall for my food and for my thirst they gave me vinegar to drink. (Ps. 69:21)

Fulfilment: They gave him sour wine mingled with gall to drink. (Mt. 27:34)

Prophecy: He guards all his bones; not one of them is broken. (Ps. 34:20)

Fulfilment: But when they came to Jesus and saw that he was already dead, they did not break his legs. (Jn. 19:33)

Prophecy: And they made his grave with the wicked – but with the rich at his death. (Is. 53:9)

Fulfilment: There came a rich man from Arimathea, named Joseph ... When Joseph had taken the body, he wrapped It in a clean cloth, and laid it in his new tomb. (Mt. 27:57-60)

When viewed in this way, the list is very impressive indeed. However, an ardent sceptic might claim that Jesus, being a good Jew, would have been aware of the Messianic prophecies that were made and so might have tried to live a life consistent with them in order to support his claim that he was the Messiah. Indeed some sceptics have tried to question the quality of the Messianic prophecies because they reject the notion that Jesus was anything more than a mere man, and they reject that idea that the Bible is the word of God. They need to question the Messianic prophecies because, if they are accepted as valid and unique, then the logical conclusion is that Jesus himself was unique and the Bible is the word of God.

The suggestion that Jesus somehow deliberately lived a life consistent with what he knew about Messianic prophecy, however, fails totally when put under the scrutiny of logic. Firstly, it is one thing to interpret these Messianic passages with hindsight now that we know that they have been fulfilled in the person of Christ, but it would have been quite another to work out beforehand just how these prophecies could be fulfilled in everyday life. Trying to live a life that fits all the details accurately would therefore be extremely difficult, if not impossible.

Secondly, had Jesus been a mere man, there would have been events in his life that were beyond his control. For example, there is no way in which he would have been able to ensure that he was born of a virgin. Neither would he have been able to guarantee the place of his upbringing or the method of his death. Had he only been a man, all these events would have happened without him being in control of the situation. It is therefore a nonsense to suggest that Jesus lived his life so that it would be consistent with the Messianic prophecies.

The ardent sceptic might still argue that the fulfilment of these Messianic prophecies might just be one enormous fluke. Theoretically, of course, something like this just might happen by chance. But the statistical probability of this is so remote as to make it virtually impossible. In order to demonstrate this we will do a little simple mathematics.

When mathematicians work out the probability of an event occurring, they use what is known as the 'product rule'. The product rule states that the probability of an occurrence of several mutually independent events is equal to the product of the probabilities that each of the given events will occur. In other words, to find the statistical probability of a series of events happening, you multiply the number of events by the probability of one of them happening by itself. This can easily be illustrated by rolling a dice.[4]

A normal dice has six sides and therefore six numbers on it. The statistical probability of throwing the dice and getting a 3 is therefore one chance in six or $1/6$. If you were to throw the dice twice, the probability of getting a three on both occasions will be the probability of the one occurrence multiplied by itself, thus $1/6 \times 1/6$, which is $1/36$. In layperson's terms, statistically there is one chance in 36 of you getting two 3's one after the other.

When we apply this product rule to the Messianic prophesies, it makes some very interesting reading. Supposing we were to think about the probability of just one of these Messianic prophecies coming true as being a $1/2$ probability. That is, it will either happen or it will not, so the situation is 50-50 ($1/2$). There is one chance in two of it actually being fulfilled. Using the same equation, the probability of just 25 prophecies being fulfilled by chance is $1/2^{25}$, or one chance in 33 million. This number is so ridiculously high it would be virtually impossible, except in the realm of theoretical mathematics, for these fulfilments of prophecy just to have happened by chance.

But two comments need to be made which dramatically increase the unlikelihood. Firstly, as we have already noted, there are many more than just 25 Messianic prophesies. Secondly, if you take a prophecy like the virgin birth, the probability of something like this happening by chance is not 50-50. Indeed if you take a representative sample of 10,000 women, the theoretical possibility of even one of them giving birth as a result of a virgin conception is nil, except of course if a miracle occurs. But even if you did give this, and other prophecies, the theoretical probability of one chance in four[5], the end result would still be $1/4^{25}$, or one chance in a thousand trillion. The reality is, Jesus' fulfilment of prophecy was no coincidence.

These were unique prophesies, they have no parallel, and they are compelling evidence of the uniqueness of the Bible and of Jesus also.

Notes

1 Ruth Tucker, *Strange Gospels*, p.128. This prophecy went so spectacularly wrong that *Awake* magazine, which is also owned by the Watchtower Society, denounced it in 1968.

2 Josh McDowell, *The New Evidence that Demands a Verdict*, p. 194.

3 And the total number of biblical prophecies would run into hundreds.

4 This argument is brilliantly expounded in John Warwick Montgomery's essay, 'Prophecy, Eschatology and Apologetics', which is part of the ETS Study *Looking into the Future*.

5 This would be a very conservative probability indeed, though it nevertheless emphasises the point more than adequately.

8

Checking up on the past

Stephen McQuoid

As we have noted from the previous chapter, the existence of numerous fulfilled prophecies makes the Bible unique. It can rightfully claim to be the word of God. But even if we accept this as the case and see that Bible both as being inspired and as being supreme among the religious books of the world, there still remain a couple of crucial issues. How do we know that the biblical text that we have in our hands has the same content as the documents that were originally penned? After all, none of the original documents exist today. And how do we know that the biblical writers really saw all that they claimed to see? This is a huge and complex issue, but we nevertheless have good reason for accepting that the documents we have are a reliable record of what took place.

This confidence can be established if we apply to the Bible the same kinds of tests that scholars of antiquity apply to any ancient document. This kind of rigour is, of course, necessary. After all, why should the Bible be allowed to bypass the work of scholarly investigation? If it is the word of God, and a book that is to be obeyed, it stands to reason that it should have the same veracity of any other ancient work.

Eyewitness Test

When scholars study any ancient text, there are a number of tests they apply to it. They firstly ask the question, did the writers really see what they claimed to see? This test could be described as the Eyewitness Test. The reason for using it is obvious. Suppose you were to come across an ancient document that claimed to be a report of the fire of Rome during the reign of Nero. The document would have a measure of credibility if it could be demonstrated that the writer lived in Rome at the time of Nero. It would have even more credibility if it could be shown that the writer was actually in Rome at the very time that the fire took place. He would be a real eye witness of the events as they unfolded. However, if the writer finished off the document by stating that he was a medieval monk living in southern Spain in the year 1256, we would have little confidence in it because we would know that he could not have been an eyewitness of the events taking place. This kind of test needs to be applied to the Bible, in particular to the Gospels as they claim to tell the historical details of the life of Jesus Christ.

Internal Test

Another test that needs to be applied is what we call the Internal Test. In this test we ask, are the copies that we have of the Bible reliable? As I have already mentioned, we do not have any of the actual documents that the biblical writers wrote on. These documents are referred to as the 'autographs', and over the span of time they have fallen into disrepair and have been destroyed. All we have is copies of the autographs. It stands to reason that we need to be sure that the copying process by which these texts have been preserved was accurate. Otherwise we will never be able to be sure that what we are reading is what was originally penned. After all, anyone who has ever played Chinese Whispers will know how easily a story can be changed as it is passed on from person to person.

External Test

A third test is what we call the External Test. In this test we ask if there is any evidence outside of a particular document that confirms some of the information that is contained in it. When applied to the Bible we ask if there are any other ancient documents that mention any of the people or places talked about in the Bible. We might even ask if there is any archaeological support that confirms what is claimed in the Bible. Again this test is entirely reasonable. If we had an ancient document in our possession that claimed many things, and then found absolutely no reference in other documents of the time to any of the things claimed, then we would have good reason to be at least a little suspicious of the content of the document.

All of these tests are useful and appropriate, and they are applied to any ancient document. If the Bible fails these tests, then we would be right to have serious questions in our minds as to the accuracy of the biblical text. If, however, the Bible passes the tests well, then we would have no reason to doubt its accuracy. This, coupled with the reasons for believing in the inspiration of the biblical text given earlier, would make a very convincing defence for the Bible as the unique word of God.

The Old Testament and the Eyewitness Test

We will begin by examining the text of the Old Testament. The first test which involves looking for eyewitness accounts does not actually apply to much of the Old Testament. Books like Proverbs, Psalms and Leviticus are not histories, so this test is simply not relevant. It does not matter if the writer of Psalm 23 was in a particular location when he penned this section of the Bible because he is not talking about any particular event. Rather he is writing poems about his experience of God. There are of course some historical sections in the Old Testament that would require eyewitness accounts and most of these can be reasonably established. The Pentateuch, for example, which contains the first five books of the Bible, was written by Moses who was personally involved in many of the key events that took place.

The Old Testament and the Internal Test

When it comes to the Internal Test which establishes the accuracy of the copies, once again the Old Testament stands up well. We can have a sense of confidence in the reliability of the copies because of the detailed copying methods that the ancient scribes used in this process.

The books of the Old Testament were generally thought to have been written on papyrus. This is a reed plant that was grown in Egypt and was then turned into writing material. The reed was sliced downwards into long thin strips and then flattened. These strips were then put at right angles to each other to form a criss-cross pattern, dried and then polished. The end product was a smooth writing surface that would have looked like a large and fairly thick page. As the material rolled easily, numerous sheets would have been pasted together and then rolled up to form a scroll. Contrary to popular perception the papyrus was very durable, but nevertheless the Jews preferred to use treated animal skin rather than papyrus when they produced their synagogue copies of the Torah (first five books of the Old Testament) as they felt it would have a longer shelf life.

All of these ancient documents were obviously handwritten. The copies of the Old Testament were produced by teams of copyists. This was an important business, and the Jews developed their own checking techniques as well as their methods of training new scribes. Being a scribe was a father-to-son occupation and the younger scribes had to be arduously apprenticed. This, however, was a very positive thing as it meant that the quality of the copying work would be of the highest order. Indeed, so sophisticated was this whole process that senior scribes became experts in the whole area of the law, and this at times brought them into dispute with Jesus. Not about their copying techniques, but about their interpretation of the law.

The Jews were aware that they were producing copies of God's word, so they took great care in the process. Copies of the Torah had to be made one at a time from another scroll. Up until the destruction of Jerusalem in AD 70, copies were made from a master copy which was kept in the temple. After this, copying took place in synagogues, each of which would have had its own master copy. Old scrolls were never thrown away, rather they would have been kept in a container called a *genizah* and often buried. Even this was a sacred business, and the burial had the reverence of a funeral. Needless to say some of these 'time capsules' have been found and have

provided valuable archaeological support for the reliability of the Old Testament text. One of the most famous
finds occurred in Cairo in 1890 and this provided scholars
with a 1,000-year-old text to work on.[1]

The copying techniques employed in the process were
complex and trustworthy. This was to ensure the preservation of an accurate text; an exact copy of the old one. For
example, once one page was copied from the original,
every line on the page was counted and compared to the
original to ensure that the copy had the same number of
lines as the original. The same thing was done with the
words and even the letters. There had to be the same number of letters on the copy as there was on the original, and
the middle letter even had to be the same on the copy as it
was in the original. If mistakes were found, the copy was
promptly destroyed. If the mistake involved one of the
names of God, the entire scroll, of which the copied sheet
was only one part, had to be destroyed. This process
appears obsessively strict, nevertheless it gives us excellent assurance of the reliability of the copying techniques.

We need to remember that these scribes would have
had remarkable memories. Unlike our modern society,
ancient ones prized memory and it was a discipline which
they worked hard at. Even today there are many Jews who
can recite the entire Torah from memory, and Muslims
who can recite the Koran. This might seem a small point,
yet it was significant. Their ability to recall information,
coupled with the copying techniques would ensure the
preservation of the Old Testament text.

The basis for the present text of the Hebrew Bible is the
Masoretic Text, and this is the prototype against which all
other texts are compared. Like other copyists before them,
the Masoretes gave painstaking detail to their work of
copying the text. As they worked on a scroll, they too
ensured that each page of the scroll was copied exactly,

line for line and word for word. They checked and cross-checked each sheet before it was sewn to the rest of the scroll. When a book was completed they subjected it to more checks including how many times each letter of the alphabet occurred in the entire scroll. Such fine attention to detail resulted in an enormously high quality text of the Old Testament.

Though we can be confident of the quality of the Masoretic Text, we can nevertheless test it for quality due to the existence of the Dead Sea Scrolls. In 1947 an Arab boy was searching for his goats among the caves of the Dead Sea region. As he threw stones into one of these caves he heard the tinkle of breaking pottery. The cave contained dozens of jars filled with the fragments of ancient documents. These were named the Dead Sea scrolls. Of the 600 scripts, 200 were biblical texts – 85 per cent of them were written on leather, the oldest of which (Exodus) was dated from 250 BC. Some of them even had footnotes stating that the manuscript was checked and found to be satisfactory. This is evidence that the Qumran community who produced the Dead Sea Scrolls were also very careful copyists. (One gets a picture of the painstaking work involved in reconstructing the Dead Sea Scrolls when realizing that there were more that 50,000 fragments in the collection).

The great significance of these scrolls is that they are 1,000 years older than the Masoretic Texts and were dated only 300 years after the close of the Old Testament canon. When the two texts were examined together, it was discovered that there was very little change. That means that over this 1,000 year gap the copying techniques had proved satisfactory and the reliability of textual transmission had been confirmed beyond all reasonable doubt.

The Old Testament and the External Test

But what of the third test for external confirmation of the contents of the document? Once again the Old Testament does very well. For example, archaeologists have come up with an almost endless list of finds that have been able to confirm the Old Testament record in numerous ways. Indeed Donald Weisman, Director of the British Museum, states that some 25,000 sites relating to Biblical times have been uncovered.[2] None of these has in any way brought into question the events, places or people mentioned in the Old Testament. On the contrary, the huge body of information which archaeologists have discovered has served only to increase confidence in the Old Testament record.

Examining the New Testament

As we look at the New Testament we can also confirm its credibility by subjecting it to the same three tests. Once again we will begin with the Eyewitness Test. This test applies particularly to the Gospel material that tells the story of the life and teachings of Jesus Christ, but it equally applies to the New Testament as a whole. It stands to reason that the credibility of the Jesus stories are greatly enhanced if those who wrote them were genuinely conversant with the events. It must also be stated that the Gospel stories are particularly important as they tell the story of Jesus who is the central figure in Christianity. If the actions and words of Jesus can in any way be verified, then they demonstrate the absolute uniqueness of Christianity, for no other religious leader or founder claimed or did anything even remotely as remarkable as the things that Jesus claimed and did.

The New Testament and the Eyewitness Test

So what evidence is there that the New Testament writers actually witnessed all the claims that they recorded? We begin by looking at the specific claims that are made. In Luke 1:1-4 the writer tells us that he had carefully recorded what was said to him by eyewitnesses. His very style is suggestive of a careful researcher and he undoubtedly gleaned his information from the many eyewitnesses who were at the scene. It is widely accepted that Mark received his information from Peter who was obviously an eyewitness to the events that took place.[3] Likewise in Galatians 1 and 2 Peter 1:16 we have claims that the writers were eyewitnesses of the events they describe. Though neither Matthew nor John explicitly claim to be eyewitnesses, the fact that they were disciples of Jesus logically indicates that they were.

It is also interesting to note that the early church highly prized eyewitness accounts, even to the point where they made eyewitness credibility a pre-requisite for apostleship, the highest rank in the church (Acts.1:21,22; Heb. 2:3). All of this demonstrates that those who wrote the New Testament, and in particular the Gospel records, were either there on the scene themselves, or obtained information from others who were on the scene. Therefore they were in a position to give evidence that would stand up in any court of law.

It is important to note the context within which Christianity emerged. Historians universally acknowledge that Christianity emerged in Jerusalem very shortly after the death and resurrection of Jesus Christ. It is clear from Acts 2 that the Christians openly proclaimed their beliefs in the public arena and in the presence of both friendly and hostile witnesses. They even proclaimed both controversial and verifiable doctrines like the resurrection of Jesus. This was controversial, not just because dead people don't rise again, but also because it was a contradiction of Jewish theology. It was verifiable because Jesus was buried in the local cemetery and the emptiness of his tomb could therefore easily be attested by visiting it. The Gospels were also circulated in the context of hostile witnesses, many of whom would have been around when the events recorded in them took place. Yet despite all of this we find no one refuting any of the claims in the gospels with any plausibility. This strongly suggests that the Gospel writers knew what they were talking about, because they were actually there or had access to eyewitnesses.

Another confirmation of the credibility of these eyewitness accounts is the fact that these followers of Jesus had nothing personal to gain from reporting what they saw. On the contrary they put themselves at great personal risk. Coming from a Jewish background where strict monotheism was upheld, their claim that Jesus was God was a complete departure from this theological tradition. In the eyes of other Jews, they were therefore risking eternal damnation in hell because of their heresy. They also were causing great offence to the Jewish religious leadership and suffered great persecution as a result. We only need to read 2 Corinthians 11:23-29 to see how severe their suffering was. Many of these early Christians, including the apostles, died a martyr's death. It is simply inconceivable that they would have been prepared to go through so much hardship if they were not absolutely convinced that their beliefs were actually true. And the truthfulness of their beliefs could only have been verified if they were actually eyewitnesses of the events recorded.

At this point we could add another test to the three that we are already using. This could be described as the 'True to History Test', though it is in some ways related to the Eyewitness Test. When historians read through an

ancient document they are looking for evidence that the
document 'rings true'. That is, they are looking for evidence of the historicity of these documents. This kind of
evidence links with the Eyewitness Test because it
strongly suggests the credibility of the eyewitness
accounts. Upon examination there are many reasons why
the Gospels ring true historically.

First of all there is the record of the way Jesus spoke.
There are many sayings attributed to Jesus that are unique
and not found anywhere else. These include his use of the
words *amen* and *abba*, his use of questions, and his use of
three-fold sayings such as 'ask and you will receive, seek
and you will find and knock and the door will be opened
to you'.[4] The uniqueness of this material strongly suggests
that these are the actual words of Jesus rather than just
some religious tradition that has been incorporated into
the gospel story. Added to this are the Aramaisms which
litter the Gospels (Aramaic words used in the text). Jesus
would have been an Aramaic speaker whereas after AD 50
most of the Christians would have been Greek speakers.
The presence of these Aramaisms suggest once more that
the material recorded was actually spoken by Jesus and
not some later tradition (which would have been entirely
in Greek) imported into the text.

Then there is the irrelevant material that is to be found
in the Gospels. If, as some scholars have suggested, the
gospel materials are a tradition that emerged in the church
towards the end of the first century, rather than the record-
ings of the life and teachings of Jesus, then the Gospels
would entirely reflect the concerns of the church at the
time. What we do find, however, is ample material that
would simply not have had any direct relevance to the
church at that time. Take for example his numerous dis-
putes with the Pharisees and the teachers of the law, as
well as the debates over such things as Sabbath and food

laws. These issues were parochial in nature and would have been irrelevant to Christians outside of Israel in the latter half of the first century. Their presence once again supports the notion that the Gospels are indeed records of what Jesus did and said.

Add to this the somewhat embarrassing material in the Gospels. The Gospels portray Jesus as a carpenter who held no political office, who was virtually a homeless wanderer, who was disliked by the authorities, was irreverent of religious practices, was in the habit of violently booting people out of the temple, had a family that distrusted him, and was followed by a bunch of cowardly failures known as the disciples. Frankly, had the church at a later date spun an account of Jesus for inclusion in the Gospels, this is a far cry from the heroic kind of figure they would have painted. The inclusion of such material gives the Gospels a resounding ring of truth.

Of course one of the reasons why some scholars doubt that the Gospels were eyewitness accounts is that they make the assumption that they were written between AD 70 and AD 95[5]. In my judgement the reasons for making these assumptions are unconvincing, whereas the reasons in favour of an earlier dating of the Gospel accounts are highly compelling. For example, one of the reasons for opting for a later date for the Gospels is the prediction that Jesus makes about the fall of Jerusalem which occurred in AD 70. Scholars who make this claim argue that Jesus could not possibly have predicted such as event, so his predictions are a story that was sewn into the material after the fall of Jerusalem had actually occurred.

This argument is only credible if the predictions are viewed from a purely naturalistic position. Indeed the argument would be compelling if we knew that predictions could not happen, that the supernatural does not exist, and that Jesus was no more than just an ordinary man. But we do not know this, indeed the evidence points in the opposite direction. This is a case of scholars coming to conclusions based on a closed-minded approach to the investigation, with inflexible and preconceived notions, as well as a lack of willingness to look at all the evidence.

If we do look honestly at the evidence we see a different picture. To get to the most important evidence for an early date for the Gospels, we must begin by looking at the book of Acts. This is because the Gospel of Luke precedes Acts, as they are part one and part two of the same work. If we get an idea of the dating for Acts, then we will know that Luke must have been written before that. We can then begin to date the other Gospels in relation to Luke.

One of the most noticeable things about the book of Acts is that it does not mention the fall of Jerusalem. This is significant as the story of both Luke and Acts centres around Jerusalem. Neither does it mention the persecutions under Nero which occurred in the mid-sixties. There is no mention of the Jewish-Roman war which erupted in AD 66. Most important of all, there is no mention of the martyrdoms of Peter (which occurred in AD 65) or Paul (which occurred in AD 64). It must be remembered that these two men are the most important figures in the book of Acts. Had Acts been written late in the first century, these events would certainly have been included, especially the martyrdoms of Peter and Paul. The exclusion of this material strongly suggests the Acts must have been completed before AD 64, and perhaps even earlier.

Bearing in mind that Acts is the second part of a two-part work, the first part, Luke's Gospel, must have been written even earlier. We also know from studying the texts of the Synoptic Gospels (Matthew, Mark and Luke) that both Luke and Matthew use material from Mark. We can logically conclude therefore that Mark is earlier than Luke. Looking at the issue chronologically, if Acts was written before AD 64, and Luke before that, and Mark before that again, then the first records of the Gospel are pushed back to very near the time of Jesus. Mark would have been in circulation while the whole generation of people (both friendly and hostile) who knew Jesus personally, were still alive. This gives further credence to the historical credibility of the Gospels.

The New Testament and the Internal Test

We now turn to the second test, the Internal Test, to see if what we now have of the New Testament is indeed what was penned all those years ago. If the copying techniques of the Old Testament scribes gives us a sense of confidence in the reliability of their transmission, then the sheer volume of New Testament documents in existence gives us the same confidence in the New Testament text.

There are some 25,000 manuscript copies of portions of the New Testament today.[6] Without doubt there are far more texts for the New Testament than there are for any other document of the ancient world. Indeed no other document even comes close. But the significance of the New Testament textual tradition lies not merely in the sheer number of manuscripts, but also in their close chronological proximity to the original manuscripts (autographs).

This point can easily be made when we compare the New Testament with the writings of Caesar, Plato and Homer. As already mentioned, there are literally thousands of New Testament texts in existence. When it comes to the writings of Caesar there are only 10 copies, of the writings of Plato there are 7 copies. Homer does better with 643 copies, but even he is a long way behind the New Testament and its 25,000 copies. The earliest fragment of a New Testament document that we have dates back to about AD 114, with the earliest books dating to AD 200.[7] That means that there is a time span of only about one hundred years between the autograph and the earliest copy. The earliest copy of the works of Caesar dates from around AD 900. The earliest copy of the works of Plato dates from AD 900, while the earliest copy of Homer's *Iliad* dates from 400 BC. That means that the time distance between the original and the earliest surviving manuscript is about a thousand years for Caesar, 1,300 years for Plato and 400 years for Homer.

Table 1: A comparison of different historic documents.

DOCUMENT	No. Copies	Earliest Copy	Time Span
New Testament	25,000	AD 200 (AD 114 Fr.)	100 years
Caesar	10	AD 900	1,000 years
Plato	7	AD 900	1,300 years
Homer	643	BC 400	400 years

Of course no credible historian would doubt the existence of Caesar, Plato or Homer, and neither would they question the general reliability of what they wrote. That being the case, to question the reliability of the New Testament would be foolish.[8] Indeed, bearing in mind the rich source of manuscripts and their proximity to the originals, if we question the reliability of the New Testament, then we would have to be consistent and cast doubt on everything we know about the ancient world.

The question that still remains, however, is how we know that what we have today still corresponds to what was written in the original manuscripts (autographs). After all, the fact that we have such a huge collection of manuscripts, however impressive this may be, in itself does not actually prove that the copying process which produced all these manuscripts is actually accurate. So how do we test the reliability of these New Testament manuscripts?

The answer to this question is actually remarkably simple, especially if you look at how the process of copying was carried out. As the New Testament began to be copied, scribes would have taken one copy, and from it they would produce several others. Each of these would in turn be taken and multiple copies made from them also. As this process continued, each new generation of manuscripts would therefore be more numerous than the previous one. Not only were more manuscripts being produced, but because Christianity was spreading, the copying process would also spread so that new copying communities would appear in new areas. Several manuscripts would be copied in Jerusalem, for example, but then taken to cities such as Antioch, Smyrna and Corinth. The manuscripts in these locations would be copied again and their copies taken to other cities further afield.

The key to testing the reliability of the copying process is to go as far back in the process as possible. If evidence of an early text can be found and compared to a more modern text, the extent of the reliability of transmission can be easily established. After all, the earlier a manuscript is, the more liable it is to be accurate. But how do we find evidence of earlier texts? The key here is to compare distant relatives.

If several manuscripts were to be found in a single location, for example Alexandria, they could be compared to each other to see if they are similar. However, it is highly probable that they were all copied from the same manuscript, so their similarities would be unsurprising and not good evidence of the reliability of the copying process over generations of copying. However, if one manuscript came from Alexandria, and another was taken from Rome, or Constantinople, or London, and compared, this would be good proof. After all, these two manuscripts would be very distant relatives, and if they were identical for all intents and purposes, then two things would be proved. Firstly, they must ultimately have come from the same source manuscript many generations ago, and secondly, the copying process was indeed reliable.

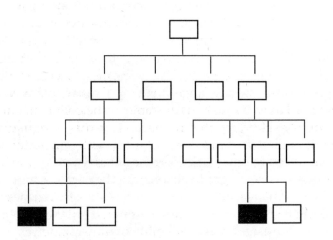

Table 2: Comparing distant relatives to find the source

Precisely this kind of test has been conducted with a great many sets of manuscripts. The sheer number of manuscripts makes this test a possibility, and we therefore have a very clear picture of just how reliable the copies that we possess really are. The embarrassment of wealth in the textual tradition, and our ability to test the manuscripts, gives us confidence in the integrity of the present New Testament text.

The New Testament and the External Test

The third test we need to think about is the External Test. Here too the New Testament passes with flying colours. In the New Testament we have numerous references to people, places and events, all of which we can then look for in other historic documents.

The writings of Jewish historian Josephus are a good place to start. He mentions numerous people and places found within the New Testament and also tells us about the trial and death of Jesus, as well as the continuation of Christianity, including the martyrdom of James the brother of Jesus. The former Rylands Professor of Biblical Criticism and Exegesis, F.F. Bruce states, 'Here, in the pages of Josephus, we meet many figures who are well known to us from the New Testament: the colourful family of the Herods; the Roman emperors Augustus, Tiberius, Claudius and Nero; Quirinias, the governor of Syria; Pilate, Felix and Festus, the prosecutors of Judea; the high-priestly families – Annas, Caiaphas, Ananias, and the rest; the Pharisees and the Sadducees; and so on. Against the background which Josephus provides we can read the New Testament with greater understanding and interest.'[9]

There are many other writings, besides those of Josephus, that we can turn to for information. Between the years of AD 70 and AD 200 the rabbis were referred to as the *Tanna' im* (repeaters of tradition). From this period there emerged a tradition known as the *Baraitha*. This was material external to the Mishnah but preserved by the Gemara. In the *Baraitha* we read about Jesus and the controversy which he caused within the Jewish establishment. It even tells us that Jesus was crucified on the eve of the Passover, which is exactly what John's Gospel tells us.[10] Further external evidence can be found among the pagan writers, the Apocrypha and miscellaneous works such as the Gospel of St Thomas.

All this compelling evidence led Sir Frederic Kenyon, formerly Principal Librarian and Director of the British Museum, a distinguished classical scholar, to write

> The Christian can take the whole Bible in his hand and say without fear or hesitation that he holds in it the true Word of God, handed down without essential loss from generation to generation throughout the centuries.[11]

All of this demonstrates persuasively that the Bible is a reliable book and one upon which we can place great confidence.

Notes

1   Terence Copley, *About the Bible*, p. 74.
2   Donald Weisman, cited in Steve Kumar, *Christianity for Sceptics* p. 111.
3   J.P. Moreland, *Scaling the Secular City*, p. 137.
4   J.P. Moreland, *Scaling the Secular City*, p.144.
5   Even if these dates for the writing of the Gospels are accepted, many of the eyewitnesses to the life of Jesus would still be alive.
6   This includes over 5,000 Greek manuscripts, 10,000 Latin Vulgate manuscripts and more than 9,000 other early versions (Josh McDowell, *The New Evidence that Demands a Verdict*, p. 34). For an important discussion on the significance of these manuscripts note the work of Bruce Metzger in *The Text of the New Testament*, chapter 2, 'Important Witnesses to the Text of the New Testament', pp. 36-92.
7   We also have a manuscript of the bulk of the New Testament from AD 250 and one of the whole New Testament from AD 325 (Josh McDowell, *The New Evidence that Demands a Verdict*, p. 38).
8   Geisler and Bocchino go as far as to claim that the New Testament is 99.9 per cent free of substantial or consequential error (*Unshakable Foundations*, p. 258).
9   F.F. Bruce, *The New Testament Documents: Are they reliable?*, p. 104.
10   F.F. Bruce, *Jesus and Christian Origins Outside the New Testament*, pp. 55, 56.
11   Sir Frederic G. Kenyon, *Our Bible and the Ancient Manuscripts*, p. 55.

Miracles or magic?

Stephen McQuoid

A number of years ago I was working on a youth project in Warrington, which involved going into schools to take RE classes and school assemblies. As it was coming up to Easter time I thought I would tell the pupils about the Easter story. This ended up being great fun and the pupils all responded well to the way I was teaching. But there is one class that stands out strongly in my mind because of a question I was asked. The pupil who asked the question did so with a smug grin on his face, which told me that he was trying to wind me up. His question, however, was an excellent one and one which many people have wrestled with. He asked, 'Do you really believe in the resurrection of Jesus and all those other miracles in the Bible?' After having thanked him for raising this important question I went on to try and answer it. But I was reminded yet again that everyone from fourteen-year-old boys to grandparents can struggle with this aspect of the Christian faith.

Of course questions about the truthfulness of the miracle stories in the Bible and elsewhere are not ones which occur in isolation. Rather they come from people who have some kind of theistic doubt. They either doubt that God exists at all, or they doubt that God could or would perform miracles. Anyone who has a firm belief in the

God of the Bible would have little problem believing in miracles because such a God is, by definition, all powerful and can work any kind of miracle. Indeed, compared to the creation of the universe, any miracle is a comparatively small thing. If you believe in a God who creates, then a God who performs the miraculous will cause you little by way of intellectual doubt.

Already in this book we have dealt with some of the evidence for the existence of God. This in itself is the most important evidence for miracles. Once you work from the assumption that an all-powerful and benevolent deity exists, then the issue of miracles will fall into place.

'Christians' questioning miracles

At this point, of course, it could be argued that even some well known 'Christians', and even members of the clergy, have questioned the reality of some of the biblical miracles. This is despite the fact that they would claim to have some kind of belief in God. I would readily concede this point. However, as Christianity is a faith which is based on the truths of the Bible, it is hard to see how anyone who does not fully accept the teachings of the Bible can truly be described as Christian. There have indeed been many church people, even leading ones who, while believing in God, have nevertheless been embarrassed by the miracle stories of the Bible and therefore question them. These I would refer to as liberal Christians, as they have a liberal attitude towards the authority of the Bible.

In general, this group would make two claims about the miracle stories. Firstly, they would claim that the miracle stories cannot be taken at face value, and therefore some other sort of explanation must be found. One of the most popular alternative explanations is to find some sort of naturalistic reason for the miracle. For example, rather than Jesus walking on water, he was actually walking on a sand bank. Such explanations, however, tend to be contrived and awkward. Furthermore, there are some miracles in the Bible that simply cannot have a naturalistic explanation. A good case in point is the raising of Lazarus (Jn. 11). This event could have no alternative explanation other than a miracle, because it involved forces outside of the natural realm. The healing of the man born blind (Jn. 9) would also need to be miraculous. Some healings have been explained away by suggesting that the disease was psychosomatic. But in this case it was congenital as he had been born blind, and so simply putting both the disease and cure down to the man's mental state is surely pushing a point too far.

Secondly, liberal Christians will insist that the truthfulness of the miracle accounts are not essential to the Christian's faith. They claim that it is perfectly acceptable to believe in the Christian gospel, and yet not to take the miracle stories at face value. Again this claim is unfounded. Take the miracles that were performed by Jesus as an example. When we read John's account of the life of Jesus, it is clear that he uses the miracle stories to attest the truthfulness of what Jesus is saying. In other words, Jesus makes all kinds of claims about himself, and then proves that those claims are true by performing a miracle. The conclusion we must come to, therefore, is that a belief in the truthfulness of miracles is essential to an authentic Christian faith, for Jesus himself used these miracles in this way. Anyone who claims to be a Christian, and yet lacks the moral courage to believe in the miracles and the intellectual courage to defend them, is denying an important aspect of the faith they claim to hold.

Of course the greatest opponents of miracles are not those who form part of the church, but those outside the church. But before we look at some of the objections that have been raised against miracles, it would be important to define exactly what we mean by a miracle. This will enable us to think about the issue more clearly.

Seeking definitions

Firstly, when we talk about miracles, we are using the word in a very specific sense. A couple of years ago I was driving through the busy city of Naples with a friend. Anyone who has ever been there will know that there are too many cars on the road going too fast, and the general standard of driving can only be described as horrendous. Once we were through the city my friend commented that it was a miracle that we had got through the city unscathed. While it was true that we had been very fortunate, this loose use of the word miracle is inadequate when talking about the miracles of the Bible. The biblical miracles were not just fortunate events, rather they were events where God broke into time and interrupted the ordinary course of things.

Secondly, biblical miracles were not just cheap conjuring tricks. As we have noted in the example of Jesus' miracles, the miracles actually attested the claims of Jesus Christ. Because they were so bound up with the ministry of Jesus and his credibility, the nature of these miracles were all-important. When Jesus performed his miracles, he did not do so for money or applause, rather they were a simple and unselfish demonstration of the power of God at work. Again when he performed the miracles they were not freakish or grotesque events. He did not give someone an extra arm or head, or even curse someone with blindness. There was nothing capricious or vulgar about them at all. Rather they were beautiful acts in which God demonstrated his purpose and love in an ordered way. They were events which helped people. They fed the hungry, healed the sick and gave sight to the blind. This puts Jesus' miracles in complete contrast to some of the alleged miraculous happenings in pagan literature.

Did they tell it like it was?

A question I am often asked is, 'How do you know the biblical writers recorded these miraculous events properly?' This question is both reasonable and fair. For if we are to look at counter arguments to miracles and then deal with them, it is important that we ensure that the thing we are arguing about is indeed factual. Just how credible are the testimony accounts for the miracles? This question has already been asked in this book in relation to the Gospel records, and answered. But with particular reference to the miracle stories found in the Gospels, Bernard Ramm lists several reasons why the testimony of the authors is adequate and reliable.[1]

Firstly, many of the miracles were done in public. Jesus did not take a few friends aside to perform miracles where no prying eyes could ask awkward questions. Rather he performed them on a hillside, in crowded towns, and in the high street, in full view of all who would pass by. It is also interesting to note that the environment in which these miracles were performed was not a controlled environment. They did not take place in a studio or theatre stage complete with props but in the open air, among the hustle and bustle of life. Despite this, we should note too that there is no record of anyone, in any of these situations, denying that a miracle had taken place.

Secondly, many of the miracles were performed in the presence of hostile witnesses. Jesus did not control the audience so that it consisted solely of devotees and the gullible. Indeed the public nature of the miracles made such an audience impossible. Often in his audience were people who bitterly opposed him and looked for a way of arranging his downfall. When the Gospel records recording the miracles were written and circulated, these same hostile witnesses were there, but again no denials of the miracles have been recorded. Furthermore, these witnesses cannot just be dismissed on the suggestion that they were primitive and gullible people and therefore could be overly impressed by a simple conjuring trick. This is because the crowds included people like the Sadducees who, far from being gullible, were utterly convinced that miracles were by their very nature impossible.

Thirdly, the miracles of Jesus were varied both in the times at which they were performed, and in the different powers that were used to carry them out. He performed miracles in lots of different places over a period of three years. When he performed the miracles he did not just do a series of miracles relating to deafness, or to blindness, or to sickness in general. What he did was to demonstrate his power over nature, disease, the spirit world, the world of knowledge, and creation itself. This great variety makes the possibility of trickery extremely unlikely.

Fourthly, there is testimony in the Gospel accounts of people having been cured. People like Lazarus, whose healing could not possibly have been psychosomatic, were healed and seen to be healed. It would have been very hard to try and convince Lazarus that he was still dead. Lazarus literally emerged from the grave to prove the reality of his healing. Therefore the historical credibility of this and other miracles could be seen every time people were able to look at Lazarus after his resurrection.

Fifthly, the miracles cannot be discounted on the basis of there being many extravagant claims of miracles in other religions. In other words you cannot just condemn the testimonies of the biblical writers as they talk about miracles, just because people from other religions also claim miracles themselves. The reason for this is that when you contrast biblical miracles with miracle claims in other religions, you are not comparing like with like. Many of the miracles claimed by other religions are believed because the devotees of that religion are believers to begin with, and the specific belief in miracles comes as a result of their prior belief. Put simply, it is because they already were believers that they believe in their miracle stories.

When it comes to the Christian miracle stories, the opposite is true. The miracle stories were there so that people would become believers. This distinction is subtle but very important. Israel as a faith community was brought into existence through a series of supernatural wonders. Jesus did not only preach about the kingdom of God, but demonstrated its power and won the hearts of many by signs and wonders. Likewise the early church experienced miracles in their time which authenticated their proclamation. All of these were designed to convince the onlookers that this faith was real. First they saw, then they believed. This order suggests that the testimonies are valid for there would be no faith if they were not. In contrast to other religions where the religion could stand even if all their miracle claims were proved false, a Christianity without the miraculous would be no Christianity at all.

Each of these pieces of evidence point to the fact that we can be confident of the testimony of those who witnessed the biblical miracles. At this point, however, someone might still object by stating that those who recorded the miracle stories were devotees of Jesus and therefore not objective. They must have put some kind of a spin on the accounts, so they cannot be taken to be reliable. This is unfair and unreasonable. It is unfair because it suggests that the fact that these people followed Jesus made them liars. It is unreasonable because the disciples of Jesus had nothing to gain by accurately reporting what they saw. Indeed they had everything to lose. In many cases they were martyred for believing in Jesus and this belief included the miracle stories.

Despite the compelling evidence for the reliability of the miracle accounts, there have nevertheless been a number of people who have raised specific objections to the biblical miracles. That being the case it is important that these objections are looked at. Naturally this cannot be an exhaustive account as space will not permit. However, I will look at the most compelling and famous arguments against miracles and deal with each in turn.

Hume and the violation of nature

The first of these comes from David Hume. Hume's basic objection stems from his perception that miracles would have to be a violation of the laws of nature and therefore an impossibility.[2] His argument takes the following path. Firstly he states that miracles by definition were a violation of nature. Next he states that the laws of nature are based on the highest degrees of probability, whilst miracles by definition must be based on the lowest degrees of probability. He therefore concludes that miracles cannot be a reality since something based on the lowest degrees of probability would be outweighed by something based on the highest degrees of probability. Miracles therefore cannot happen, and in the case of the miracles that are reported in the Bible, they did not happen.

In dealing with this argument I would want to point out that I actually agree with some aspects of it. For example, I would readily acknowledge that natural law is based on a high degree of probability. This is self-evident. Experience would tell us that there are four seasons: summer, autumn, winter and spring. We know this because they occur in that order every year. We would therefore expect winter in any given year to follow autumn because there is an enormous probability that this will be the case.

Equally I would agree that the idea of a miracle is based on a low probability. Indeed if miracles were probable and expected, they would almost certainly cease to be miracles. It is because they are not the norm, because they are unusual and unexpected events, that we call them miracles.

At this point, however, the agreement with Hume ceases, and does so for two reasons. Firstly, I would contend with the use of the word 'violation' in his argument. If by this Hume merely means that a miracle is a supernatural event which is therefore different from the normal run of events then I would be happy. But this is not what he means. By violation, Hume means that there is an inviolable law of nature that cannot change because the natural order depends on it. Indeed, Hume would argue, the natural order would come to an end if such a violation occurred, therefore miracles cannot happen. This however is absurd. After all, how do we know that natural laws exist? We know by observation. We look at the evidence and conclude what the norm is. But in order to be as dogmatic about natural law as Hume is, one must have looked at all the evidence, including the evidence that suggests that miracles, a departure from the norm, have occurred. But Hume does not do this. He merely makes his dogmatic statement about the laws of nature, and then dismisses all the evidence for miracles because they do not fit into his argument. This position is intellectually unjustifiable.

If Hume were to have been more honest, and his research more thorough, he would not have concluded that a miracle such as the resurrection could not have occurred because it would be a violation on some inviolable natural law. Rather he would have concluded that people who are dead usually do not rise again from the dead, but history demonstrates that there is one notable exception to this rule. We should therefore not expect that resurrection from the dead will be a common occurrence; probability tells us that it will not be, but that the miracle of resurrection is possible, even though improbable. This is a more balanced position because it takes all the evidence into account rather that relying on some sort of naturalistic bias.

I would also contend with Hume on a second issue. This is related to what I have already stated. Theoretical probabilities should never be allowed to outweigh actual evidence! Hume comes to his conclusion about miracles entirely because he trusts in theoretical probability. This is unsustainable.

I love playing cards, and I confess that there are few things in a card game as thrilling as looking at a hand of cards and realising that you have the capability of winning the game, even before it begins. However, it is unlikely that I would ever be dealt such a hand. Note I said unlikely, not impossible. In the game of bridge, for example, the chances of being dealt a perfect hand are 1 in 635,013,559,600.[3] This scenario is extremely unlikely. But anyone who plays cards regularly will know that it does actually happen. Indeed if someone trustworthy told me that he had a perfect hand, it would be ludicrous for me to disbelieve him, just because the mathematical probability is so slight. But this is exactly what Hume does.

In the New Testament we have four accounts of the miracle stories. These accounts are given by four honest, sober and sane people who had nothing to gain and everything to lose by telling their story. Even though the probability of these miracles occurring is slight, nevertheless the testimony of those who were witnesses to the miracles should outweigh the mathematical improbability of them occurring. Seen in this light, Hume's objections are weak at best.

Hume and counter miracles

Hume has one further objection to miracles. This is the issue of the presence of counter miracles.[4] He notes that religions, other than Christianity, also claim miracles which are in support of their truth claims. However, if one religion contradicts another, but both claim miracles, then the miracles must be discounted as evidence, because such a contradiction cannot exist.

In this regard Hume is quite correct. All 'like' or 'equal' miracles do in fact cancel each other out, and would invalidate each other as evidence for a truth claim. However, far from being a supposed nail in the coffin of Christianity, this actually supports the Christian case. This is because Christianity alone is supported by unique and unequalled miracles which no other religion can match, either in their display of power or the evidence with gives these claims credibility. For example, Islamic tradition claims some miracles, for example that Mohammed healed the broken leg of a companion. But these are mentioned in the Hadith rather than the Koran.[5] This tradition comes hundreds of years after the death of Mohammed which means that the record of these miracles is not based on eyewitness accounts, like the Gospels, but merely on uncorroborated later tradition.

Hume has therefore not damaged Christianity; he has unwittingly highlighted one of its strengths. The fact is

that no other religion can come up with a miracle as spec-
tacular as the resurrection of Christ, which can be historically proved beyond all reasonable doubt. Therefore no
other religion can use miracles as a justification of their
truth claim, but Christianity can.

Antony Flew and repeatable events

Another sceptic who has written on the subject of miracles
is Antony Flew. Flew's argument is in many ways similar
to that of Hume.[6] He states that miracles are particular and
unrepeatable events whereas the laws of science describe
general and repeatable events. His conclusion is that the
evidence for general and repeatable events is far greater
than the evidence for particular and unrepeatable events,
and the weaker evidence should be discounted. For Flew,
therefore, miracles should not be believed.

In this argument Flew is not actually ruling out the possibility of miracles, rather he is just ruling out their believ-
ability. However his argument still fails the test of logic.
Before we look at the reasons for this, we need to concur
with Flew that miracles are indeed particular and unrepeatable events. If they were not then they would be part
of the natural order and therefore not miracles.

As for the rest of Flew's argument, it leaves much to be
desired. Firstly, it is wrong to say that the evidence for the
general and repeatable will always be greater than evidence for the particular and unrepeatable. Like Hume,
Flew has jumped the gun and passed sentence on the
miraculous before the evidence has been fully investigated. This is as logically flawed as the approach taken by
Hume. Secondly, just as Hume could easily have been presented with good historical evidence for miracles, so too
could Flew. Miracles are indeed particular and

unrepeatable, but if the evidence suggests that they happened, then it is ridiculous to discount them just because they do not fit the general and repeatable criteria of the natural world. In the end, Flew's argument is as weak and unimpressive as Hume's.

Guy Robinson and the elimination of miracles

Another attack on the miraculous comes from scientific naturalists such as Guy Robinson.[7] He argues that science by its very nature declares that all events are explicable on the basis of science. In other words, every event must be naturalistic so that it can have a scientific explanation. Miracles however are not naturalistic and therefore cannot be explained on the basis of science. As a result miracles cannot exist.

Robinson's argument is as flawed as the previous two, and with no redeeming features. Firstly, it must be pointed out that Robinson's position is profoundly anti-supernatural as opposed to being objective. He limits everything to a scientific explanation and this automatically discounts anything which is not scientifically explicable, irrespective of any evidence to the contrary. Secondly, there is no reason why science must assume naturalism. Indeed, given the existence of evidence for non-naturalistic realities, it is better scientific practice to admit that our present models of science have their limitations. A good scientist will not only look at naturalistic explanations for what he sees, but for the best explanation, which will not necessarily be naturalistic. Science is confined to the realms of the physical so it is an abuse of science to use it in order to make metaphysical judgements. Robinson's problem is that he has backed himself into a corner, and in doing so has limited his ability to understand the miraculous at all.

Alastair McKinnon and the impossibility of miracles

A fourth objection to the miraculous comes from Alastair McKinnon who believed that the natural course of events makes miracles impossible.[8] He argues that a natural happening is something that occurs in the natural course of events. Miracles however are not part of the natural course of events, indeed they are contrary to it. But nothing can exist that is not part of the natural course of events. This is because all that exists is that which is part of the natural course of events.

Once again this is a leap in logic. Certainly it is true to say that all natural events are part of the natural course of events, but there is no evidence that all events are part of the natural course of events and no way of proving this is the case. What is more, just because something cannot be explained by the natural course of events, that does not mean that it is not real, or that it cannot occur within the natural course of events. Miracles can therefore take place within the natural world even though the natural course of events cannot explain them. To deny this is simply to reveal one's anti-supernatural bias. McKinnon does exactly this, and like the others mentioned, is guilty of doing so without looking objectively at all the evidence.

It is interesting when surveying all these objections to miracles that the objectors do not produce any historical or actual proof that miracles did not and cannot happen. Rather they create their own hypotheses which will automatically discount the miraculous. However, as none of them have actually looked honestly at the evidence for miracles or taken it seriously, they are guilty of an anti-supernatural bias which renders objective examination impossible. They would, of course, all argue that the theist also approaches the issue with a theistic bias. While this is true, at least the theist can justify his position with the evidence. Indeed he comes to his position because of the evidence. This is a better position that ignoring the evidence and relying on prejudice.

In the end the evidence for miracles is very compelling. The ball is in the sceptics' court. If they wish to be taken seriously, they must interact with all the evidence and not just try to win the argument on the basis of their anti-supernatural bias. This is simply not good enough.

Notes

1   Bernard Ramm, *Protestant Christian Evidences*, pp.140-143.
2   David Hume, *An Enquiry Concerning Human Understanding*, sec. X, pt. I.
3   Norman Geisler uses this argument against Hume very convincingly (Norman Geisler, *Christian Apologetics*, p. 267).
4   David Hume, *Enquiry,* sec. X, pt. II.
5   Lee Strobel, *The Case for Faith*, pp. 70,71.
6   Antony Flew, 'Miracles', *Encyclopaedia of Philosophy*, vol. 5, pp. 346-353.
7   Guy Robinson, *Miracles*, Ration 9 pp. 155-166, cited in Norman Geisler, *Christian Apologetics*, p. 271.
8   Alastair McKinnon, 'Miracle', American Philosophical Quarterly 4, pp. 308-314.

10

More than a man

Alastair Noble

Here's a tragic Christmas incident to ponder. A church worker was telling a class of infants in a Scottish school the Nativity story. When he described how Mary and Joseph called the new born baby 'Jesus', one of the pupils asked why they gave their son a swear word for a name.

Such is the educational and cultural progress of our time that the name of the Founder of the Faith which underpins our civilisation is best known as a coarse conjunction in our conversation. Christ features regularly as an expletive in radio and television dramas, with the claim, if challenged, that it adds to the credibility of the language. Now there's a thought: blasphemy as authenticity.

I rather doubt that name of the Founder of Islam, or of any other world religion for that matter, would get such treatment. If we're not removing the name of Jesus from our culture so as not to offend, we're demonstrating our broadmindedness by using it as an oath, even though it is revered by millions of people around the world. We need to wake up to consequences of destroying everything that is sacred in our culture and tolerating such religious vandalism as an expression of our sophistication.

What is it about Jesus?

When I was in South Korea recently, I was deeply impressed by the number of churches I saw. It was particularly impressive at night when the neon crosses on each church were lit up and you sensed that this was an increasingly Christian country. In fact, 25 per cent of the population are now professing Christians, a position that has developed from only a handful 50 years ago. What is it that attracts enthusiastic, busy, efficient, hard-working people to a faith that is centred in the events of a single life lived out 2,000 years ago?

In Angola, I saw the same thing, but in very different circumstances. Here's a country that has been devastated by almost thirty years of civil war and suffered many thousands of deaths; a country where poverty and ill health are the common lot of the vast majority of the people. But why are there still so many churches? Why an increasing number of Christians? Why a continuing respect for the missionaries who brought the message of Jesus in colonial times?

There is unquestionably something highly durable about Jesus Christ. The Bolsheviks were determined to impose atheism on Russia after the 1917 revolution, but the last ever May Day Parade in the now defunct USSR was especially notable for the presence of Orthodox Church groups carrying a large wooden crucifix! Hitler declared his intention of destroying the Catholic Church in Germany as soon as the war was won, but he didn't even get to start with that initiative. The first Communist President of independent Angola said that he expected that his country would be rid of Christianity within a generation. He's gone now, but not the church.

Why does allegiance to Jesus Christ grow, often expo-nentially, when dictators persecute the church? What is it about this individual that commands such loyalty from people, even under the most extreme pressure? How is it that two billion people in the world today claim some commitment to Jesus Christ? Why is our calendar based on the date of his birth? How did a first century homeless Galilean carpenter turned teacher, who had only 12 disciples at the beginning, achieve this level of historical dominance and international acceptance?

The historical facts

Incredible as it may seem, it has occasionally been fashion-able to deny the actual historical existence of Jesus and claim that he was a figment of the imagination of some over enthusiastic idealists in the second or third centuries AD. Happily, no serious scholar of Christian history would now accept such a proposition.

The New Testament of the Bible provides a remarkably full and consistent account of the life and teaching of Jesus of Nazareth which can stand, in its own right, the rigours of historical analysis. In addition, a number of references to Jesus are to be found in non-biblical documents. Although relatively few, they are from a variety of sources and are of considerable interest. For example, the Jewish historian Flavius Josephus in his work *The Antiquities of the Jews*, published in AD 93, makes the comment, 'And there arose about this time Jesus, a wise man, if indeed we should call him a man: for he was a doer of marvellous deeds, a teacher of men.' Another reference is found in a letter from Pliny the Younger, the governor of Bithynia in Northern Turkey, to the Emperor Trajan in the year AD 112. Writing about the Christians he encountered, he noted that 'they were in the habit of meeting on a certain day before it was light, when they sang an anthem to Christ as God, and bound themselves by a solemn oath not to commit any wicked deed.' The Roman historian, Cornelius Tacitus, governor of Asia Minor around the same time, observed that 'Christus, from whom they got their name, had been executed by sentence of the procurator Pontius Pilate, when Tiberius was emperor.'

F.F. Bruce, the great British New Testament scholar, draws this conclusion from the non-biblical evidence about Jesus. 'Whatever else may be thought of the evidence from early Jewish and Gentile writers, ... it does at least establish, for those who refuse the witness of Christian writings, the historical character of Jesus Himself.'[1] The life of Jesus is at the very least as certain as the existence of Julius Caesar. And his impact on the subsequent history of the world is considerably greater!

Astonishing claims

The real issue about Jesus is not whether he lived or not, but how we should respond to the claims he made about himself. When examined carefully, they are truly remarkable.

There is near universal agreement that Jesus is among the handful of people who have decisively altered the course of human history. He is regarded as one of the world's great teachers and a supreme example of all that is morally desirable. He is always placed among the founders of the great world religions, alongside figures like Buddha, Confucius, Krishna and Mohammed. But, in fact, Jesus' life and his claims about himself stand out in stark contrast to their experiences and teaching. All of them, in varying degrees, admit to their own imperfections and none claimed to be God incarnate. Indeed, their struggles and shortcomings were the basis of many of their claims to have deeper insight into the human predicament. That Jesus' actions and teachings are so different from theirs is either a very awkward anomaly for Christianity or the unavoidable reason for believing that he is who he claimed to be and, therefore, absolutely unique among the great figures of the earth.

Many people recognise the attractiveness and impact of the life and teaching of Jesus, but hesitate to accept that he is anything more than an outstanding human figure. The idea that he is God come into the world – God incarnate – is, for them, a step too far. But this is where we encounter a serious difficulty. We do not normally admire people who talk about themselves and make extravagant claims about their own personal status. We usually find that sort of thing highly embarrassing. So, when we find that the claims Jesus made for himself are truly breathtaking, how are we to respond? If his assertions are not true, then in no sense can he or his teaching be admired. If they are true, then they cannot be ignored!

Steve Kumar has provided a helpful summary of Jesus' claims about himself.[2] He shows that Jesus claimed to

- forgive sin – see Matthew 9:1-8
- judge the world – see John 5:27-30
- give eternal life – see John 3:16
- be sinless – see John 8:46
- be the object of faith – see John 8:24
- answer prayer – see John 14:13, 14
- be worthy of worship – see Matthew 14:33
- be the Truth – see John 14:6
- have all authority – see Matthew 28:18
- be in essence one with God – see John 10:30.

It is frequently asserted that Jesus never claimed to be God. But any serious reading of the New Testament will quickly dispel that notion. He certainly did, and regularly too. It is also highly speculative to argue, as for example Geza Vermes has done recently,[3] that the disciples, to borrow the now infamous phrase, 'sexed up the dossier' of Jesus' teaching to make him appear divine and the content of his teaching more credible. You might be tempted to do that with secret intelligence information, but not with inspired teaching given to thousands of people in public! Such an approach begs the question as to why you would want to believe such an unlikely construction of a rather more obvious truth.

The claims of Jesus about himself are really not negotiable. If he is who he claimed to be, then he is the Supreme Figure of History and he holds the key to every question of our existence. If his claims are not true, then he and his teaching should be utterly rejected as delusional and destructive fantasies. Few of those who deal in condescending platitudes about Jesus and his teaching have ever really understood the stark nature of that choice.

C.S. Lewis, Professor of Mediaeval and Renaissance Literature at the University of Cambridge and a great Christian apologist, has given the clearest statement of the dilemma: 'A man who ... said the sort of things Jesus said would not be a great moral teacher. He would either be a lunatic – on the level with the man who says he is a poached egg – or else he would be the Devil of Hell. You must make your choice. Either this man was, and is, the Son of God: or else a madman or something worse. You can shut Him up for a fool, you can spit at Him and kill Him as a demon; or you can fall at His feet and call Him LORD and God.'[4] I think that says it all!

Did they all get it wrong?

It is astonishing how quickly the message about the death and resurrection of Christ spread throughout the Roman Empire. Within weeks thousands of people had become Christians in Jerusalem, the very city where the drama was played out and where, if there had been any doubt about the validity of the message, it would have been quickly detected.[5] Within a few years, key cities like Antioch, Thessalonica and Ephesus had become centres of Christian mission.[6] Within a few decades, there was a church in Rome, the imperial capital of the Empire, and churches as far away as North Africa. Within a century or so the message about Jesus was being heard as far away as Spain and southern Britain in the West and India in the East.

And the early Christians had no doubts about who Jesus is. For example, this early Christian hymn or poem, which summarises much of their beliefs about Jesus, is quoted in the New Testament.

Your attitude should be the same as that of Christ Jesus:
Who, being in very nature God,
  did not consider equality with God something to be grasped, but made himself nothing,
  taking the very nature of a servant,
  being made in human likeness.
And being found in appearance as a man,
  he humbled himself and became obedient to death – even death on a cross!
Therefore God exalted him to the highest place
  and gave him the name that is above every name,
that at the name of Jesus every knee should bow,
  in heaven and on earth and under the earth,

and every tongue confess that Jesus Christ is Lord,
to the glory of God the Father.[7]

What is striking about these words is that they identify
Jesus as God and give him the revered title 'LORD',
reserved in the Jewish faith only for Jehovah, the Creator
of the World and the only true God of Israel. And it is
worth bearing in mind that many of the first Christians
had been devout Jews. In addition, to confess any other
Lord than Caesar was, in Roman society, to risk, at the
very least, being ostracised and at worst, being executed.
The early Christians understood the overriding importance of confessing Jesus as LORD, despite the potential for
martyrdom it carried with it. It is also noteworthy that the
passage demands for Jesus the worship implied in 'confessing' and 'bowing the knee' that was the sole right of
Almighty God.

It is also impressive that the people who knew Jesus
best, both before the crucifixion and after the resurrection,
had no doubts about his uniqueness and about his claim to
be God incarnate. For example, Peter, the impetuous fish-
erman, who was in the inner circle of Jesus' disciples
records that 'He committed no sin'.[8] John, who was particularly close to Jesus, writes that 'in him is no sin.'[9] And
Paul, whose towering intellect gave the Christian message
its first complete exposition, concludes that he 'had no
sin'.[10] A remarkable triple testimonial! No wonder the
apostles from the very beginning were convinced of the
distinctiveness of Christ and that he was the ultimate revelation of God to the world. 'Salvation is found in no-one
else, for there is no other name under heaven given to men
by which we must be saved', is how Peter declared their
new-found faith.[11]

And we cannot ignore the colossal impact of Jesus
Christ on the subsequent history of our planet. In his

remarkable book *The Need to Believe*, first published in 1959, Professor Murdo Macdonald describes the influence of Christ and his teaching on the development of democracy and political systems, on the progress of social reform, and in culture and the arts. He concludes: 'The history of Western civilisation is inexplicable apart from Jesus Christ. When due place is given to the influence of Greek culture, Roman law and administrative genius, His is by far the dominating influence. The Carpenter of Nazareth, denounced by His own people, destroyed by His enemies, has become the Supreme personality of all time ...'[12] Nearer home, the recognition by some that the British Labour Movement owes much more to Christ and Methodism than to Marx and Marxism is a further case in point. The impact of Christ on every aspect of civilisation is certainly inescapable and demands serious consideration.

Now in flesh appearing

Thus goes the line in the beloved Christmas carol, sung each year with such enthusiasm but often without much understanding. It goes directly to the heart of the Christian message.

At some point in their lives, most people ask themselves how, if God exists, he can be known. How does he reveal himself? Is it in dreams, visions or voices? Or in natural phenomena, in catastrophes, in music and the arts, in silence or in deafening sound? The answer is more wonderful than could have been imagined. While God does make himself known in a variety of ways, he has chosen to make the most complete revelation of himself by being born into the world and living within it in the person of Jesus Christ.

When I worked as an inspector of schools, teachers would remind me occasionally that I didn't know what the reality of the job was like as I had not been in the classroom for years. It was not a wholly convincing argument as I had worked in schools for a considerable period of time! So, if you accept the Christian doctrine of the Incarnation – the coming of God into the world in human form in Christ– you can't accuse God of not knowing at all what the world is like! Of course, because he is the Creator, he is bound to know anyway. But just consider how much more authentic his actual presence in the world makes his revelation to us.

There is nothing inherently improbable about God choosing to enter his own world by the process of birth, experiencing at firsthand the joys of childhood and the responsibilities of manhood, so that we can understand something of his purposes. But such a method of revelation requires authentication. And that is precisely what we have. The whole tenor of Christ's life is utterly exceptional. His birth and life are characterised by the momentous and the miraculous. And the ultimate proof that Jesus is God lies in his actual resurrection from the dead, a subject to which we shall turn in the next chapter.

Crucified under Pontius Pilate

But we have to face one other perplexing reality. If Jesus is God and if he deliberately chose to enter this world, why was crucifixion a crucial part of the plan? Put simply, why is the cross the enduring symbol of Christianity?

In reading the record of Jesus' life in the New Testament, it quickly becomes apparent that the crucifixion of Jesus was not, by any stretch of the imagination, an unexpected development. It was predicted in his infancy;[13]

described in his ministry;[14] and identified as his destiny.[15] It gradually became clear that many of the prophecies of the Old Testament which described the suffering of the Messiah foreshadowed Jesus' death.[16] The apostolic message of the gospel – the good news for the nations – was focused on the crucifixion of Jesus.[17] The inescapable conclusion, therefore, is that the death of Jesus not only became the central truth of the Christian message by virtue of the course of events but also because it was designed to be so by a Higher Hand.

Very occasionally, someone convicted of murder, or one of their relatives, will argue that the death penalty is preferable to life imprisonment. And methods of execution, however dreadful to contemplate, have generally become, in our world, more humane. But for anyone to accept the necessity to die by Roman crucifixion,[18] given its sheer brutality and indescribable torture, is truly remarkable. Yet this is what Jesus did and it begs the question why he should do so.

Ever since I was a child I have wondered why it was necessary that Jesus had to die. Surely, I often thought, there could have been some other way by which the wrongs of the world could be put to right. But there are several crucial dimensions of the death of Jesus and when they are taken together we begin to see its necessity and significance.

• Firstly, the sheer injustice of the crucifixion of Jesus conveys a message about what our world is really like and what human beings are capable of. That Jesus represents the highest and best in human experience is universally acknowledged. That he was completely innocent of the crimes of which he was accused was acknowledged even by the Roman Governor who ordered his crucifixion – an utterly bizarre and intolerable situation.[19] That his death was ordered for reasons of political and religious expediency was apparent from the very start of his imprisonment.[20] Such is the universal recognition of the massive injustice of the crucifixion of Jesus that we frequently refer to people being 'crucified' in situations where they become the scapegoat for the errors of others. The first truth, then, is that the cross tells us something about ourselves.

- Secondly, if Jesus is God, then the crucifixion carries a powerful message about God's attitude to us. He not only cares about us, but is willing to go to the almost unbelievable extremes of human suffering in order to demonstrate his love for us and to experience the real suffering of the world in which we are all caught to some extent. The second truth has to be that the cross tells us something about the nature of God.

- Thirdly, for reasons that are ultimately deeply mysterious, it takes the suffering and death of Jesus to touch our emotions at the deepest level and draw us to God. It is almost as if it is necessary for us to face up to the misery and rebellion of the world that is encapsulated in the cross before we can begin the journey of faith and recover our relationship with the Creator. Just as, at the end of the Second World War, large numbers of German civilians were obliged to witness the horrors produced by the concentration camps in order to demonstrate the desperate consequences of Nazism, so we need to understand the suffering of the cross to deliver us from our innate selfishness. The third truth about the cross, then, is that it tells us something about the nature of forgiveness and faith.

Taking up the cross

The one thing you would have to say about Jesus is that he could never be accused of 'spin' in the message he brought to the world. His insistence that his followers should take up the cross and follow him[21] is not the most promising material for advertising executives. 'Gallows as Lifestyle' does not immediately seem to be an attractive selling point. And yet that is precisely how Jesus and his apostles declared the gospel – and were not afraid to call it 'good news'.

So how do we truly become followers of Jesus? Well, firstly, it is necessary to accept the message of the cross. It demonstrates the nature of the world's rebellion against God and emphasises that we are all, to some degree, involved in it. If God's Son was so utterly rejected when he came into the world, there is a problem at the heart of human experience which touches each one of us. The cross calls for repentance – the willingness to acknowledge our sin and rebellion and to turn away from it.

The late Tom Allan, minister of St George's Tron Church in Glasgow, had a remarkable conversion story which illustrates this very point. Serving with British Forces in France during World War Two, he had become disillusioned with the Christian faith in which he had been brought up. But in 1945 a close friend, an American officer, invited him to attend the Easter service in Rheims Cathedral. He went reluctantly, out of respect for his col-league. He was quite detached from the ceremony until a soldier sang the well-known spiritual, 'Were you there when they crucified my LORD?' Tom Allan's first thought was that it was utterly ridiculous to suggest he was there. How could he have been there 2,000 years ago? But gradually it dawned on him that his agnostic way of life was entirely consistent with the attitude of the multitude of people who shouted for the crucifixion of Jesus or just simply stood by and let it happen. That thought depressed him deeply until he realised that, if he was there when the Lord was crucified, he must also have been there when Jesus prayed, 'Father, forgive them, for they do not know what they are doing.'[22] The realisation that Jesus prayed for his personal forgiveness transformed his life and made him the great Christian preacher and social activist that he became.

Secondly, we need to accept the expression of God's love to us. We may be rebellious, wilful and unattractive people. But God's desire to reach us has no limit. He has given himself in Jesus to rescue us from ourselves and from the seductiveness of the world. Jesus has paid the ultimate price to bring us to our senses and provide the means of forgiveness and healing. In the cross, God says through Jesus that he is willing to accept us as we are – to take us back![23]

And thirdly, we need to believe that only in the death of Jesus is the means of our forgiveness and salvation. Just as there are truths about the natural world which go beyond rational analysis, so there are mysteries about the cross that defy explanation. But its central message is this. In his death, Jesus, who is sinless, takes to himself the consequences of our sin and, if we accept his sacrifice for us in faith, we are forgiven.[24] Turning to God in repentance and having faith in Jesus Christ is the core message of Christianity.[25]

Some years ago, at the height of the troubles in Northern Ireland, a bomb was exploded one morning under a car in a quiet London suburb. Intended to assassinate an MP, it killed, in error as so often is the case in terrorist outrages, a leading surgeon whose life was dedicated to working with children with cancer. The public revulsion that followed became part of the growing realisation that this was no way to resolve political problems and it contributed in some measure to the quest for a solution. It was abundantly clear that the distinguished surgeon died because of the sin committed by the terrorists who planted the bomb – a sin for which they are ultimately responsible before God – and for no other reason.

It is obvious that Jesus died because of the sins of those who were involved in his crucifixion. They included the political and religious leaders, as well as the vocal mobs and silent groups which were part of the grisly drama. What can also be said about the death of Jesus and about no other is that he died not only because of sin but also *for* sin. His death is unique in that it is truly substitutionary. His sufferings cancel our sins. His death contains the means of our forgiveness. St Paul was absolutely clear about this: 'Christ died for our sins'.[26]

When we open our mind to the meaning of the cross and accept its message in faith, we take the first steps to making the cross the rule of our lives and the inspiration for service to Christ and others. This is certainly 'taking up the cross' and accepting everything it brings. And as with all the challenges the Christian message brings, what other choices do we have?

In his delightful book, *The Incomparable Christ*, John Stott recounts a story about Sundar Singh, an affluent Sikh, who became a Christian at considerable cost to himself in terms of his relationship with his family and community. On one occasion while visiting a Hindu college, a lecturer rather aggressively asked him what particular principle or doctrine he had found in Christianity which had led to his conversion. 'The particular thing I have found,' replied Sundar Singh, 'is Christ.'[27]

When we acknowledge Jesus as Lord and give him our allegiance, we are not just embracing an idea or reaching out for an ideal. It is more even than committing ourselves to study his teachings and spread his gospel. We are actually accepting his absolute uniqueness and recognising that he is, to the exclusion of all others, God become man and the Saviour of the world. I do hope you see that for yourself!

Notes

1   F.F. Bruce, *The New Testament Documents*, p. 119.
2   Steve Kumar, *Christianity for Sceptics* – this book has been particularly helpful in writing this chapter.
3   Geza Vermes, *The Authentic Gospel of Jesus.*
4   C.S. Lewis, *Mere Christianity.*
5   See, for example, Bible, New Testament, Acts 2:41; 6:7.
6   See, for example, Bible, New Testament, Acts 11:19-30; 13:1-4.
7   Bible, New Testament, Phil. 2:5-11.
8   See Bible, New Testament, 1 Pet. 2:22.
9   See Bible, New Testament, 1 Jn. 3:5.
10 See Bible, New Testament, 2 Cor. 5:21.
11 See Bible, New Testament, Acts 4:12.
12 Murdo Macdonald, *The Need to Believe.*
13 See, for example, Bible, New Testament, Lk. 2:34,35.
14 See, for example, Bible, New Testament, Mt.16:21-23.
15 See, for example, Bible, New Testament, Jn. 11:23-33.
16 See, for example, Bible, New Testament, Lk. 24:25-27.
17 See, for example, Bible, New Testament, 1 Cor. 1:17-19.
18 See, for example, Bible, New Testament, Mk. 10:45.
19 See, for example, Bible, New Testament, Lk. 23:13-25.
20 See, for example, Bible, New Testament, Jn. 18:14.
21 See, for example, Bible, New Testament, Mt. 16:24-28.
22 See, for example, Bible, New Testament, Lk. 23:34.
23 See, for example, Bible, New Testament, 1 Pet. 2:24,25.
24 See, for example, Bible, New Testament, Jn. 3:16.
25 See, for example, Bible, New Testament, Acts 20:21.
26 See, for example, Bible, New Testament, 1 Cor. 15:3.
27 John Stott, *The Incomparable Christ*, p. 16.

11

Dead men stay dead: or do they?

Alastair Noble

When Harry Truman, the American President, was briefed on the extent of the damage caused by the first atomic bomb dropped on Hiroshima in August 1945 at the end of World War Two, he exclaimed excitedly, 'This is the greatest thing in history!' He probably changed his view in the light of subsequent world events, but at the time he was no doubt mightily relieved that America had a weapon which would ensure the end of the costly Pacific War and which might even make war unthinkable in the future.

Interestingly, a BBC Radio survey at the time of the millennium celebrations in 2000 found that the listeners thought that the use of atomic weapons in 1945 was the most significant news story of the twentieth century. The 1969 moon landing came a close second. But it is unthinkable that anyone would now seriously propose that the use of these weapons in 1945 was the greatest thing in history.

What is the greatest thing in history?

It is intriguing to consider whether any event in history merits being described as the greatest. There certainly have been significant turning points in history which have determined the fate of nations for better or worse. Some battles, like El Alamein in North Africa in 1942, have had a decisive effect on the course of military campaigns. A number of discoveries have opened up new continents or brought huge benefits to the lives of millions of people. But it is almost impossible to select one event which can be described as the most important of them all.

And yet Christians have no difficulty with this challenge. For them there is no question that there is a single event in history which transcends all others in its importance and impact. That event is the resurrection of Jesus Christ. It occurred just after the Jewish Passover, around the year AD 33. The actual date is much less important than the event itself which, coming three days after the execution of Jesus by Roman crucifixion, is truly miraculous. The one-third of the world's population who claim, in varying degrees, to be followers of Christ, and the annual celebration in churches in almost every country of the resurrection of Jesus each year at Easter are powerful testimonies to the abiding significance of this event for many millions of people.

The resurrection of Jesus

For many people, of course, the resurrection of Jesus raises a number of questions and not least whether it happened at all. In this chapter we shall explore the evidence for and some of the objections to the resurrection of Jesus Christ. But before we get to that, it is important to be clear about the central place of the resurrection in the Christian message. Although it is fashionable for some modern theologians and church leaders to regard belief in the actual resurrection of Jesus as an optional extra, this was certainly not the view of the apostles of Christ and of the first Christians.[1]

In fact, the disciples of Jesus were driven somewhat reluctantly to accept that Jesus had risen from the dead. At first they were just as sceptical as any modern cynic. Indeed some of them were utterly dismissive of the first reports brought to them and were only convinced by the irrefutable presence of the risen Christ among them.[2] St Paul, the great exponent of the gospel of Christ to the Roman world was, before his conversion, a determined persecutor of the Christians because he regarded their faith as a destructive perversion of Judaism. Then he had a personal encounter with Jesus, on the proverbial road to Damascus, and such was the transformation in his thinking that he was later to insist, '… if Christ has not been raised, your faith is futile.'[3]

Some recent surveys of religious belief in Britain show that there is considerable confusion about the significance of the resurrection of Jesus. The 2001 National Census revealed that 72 per cent of people in Britain consider themselves to be Christians. However, a sample survey carried out by a national newspaper for Easter 2003 revealed that only 49 per cent believed in the resurrection. Add to this the recent data about church attendance in Britain at around 10 per cent and you wonder what place the resurrection of Jesus has in the thinking of many professing Christians. A substantial proportion, it seems, feel they can claim to be Christians without believing that Jesus rose from the dead. Even more seem to be able to accept the most dramatic event at the heart of Christianity without feeling the need to celebrate it and explore its implications in church.

The first Christians had no such misgivings. It was the preaching of the resurrection which brought them to faith in Jesus Christ as Saviour and Lord and released them from a multitude of pagan superstitions. It authenticated for them the teaching of Jesus and clarified the meaning of his crucifixion. It filled their lives with a sense of purpose and direction. And ultimately, only the resurrection delivered them from the fear of dying and gave them a certain hope for the world beyond.[4]

It is necessary, therefore, to examine the contemporary evidence on which such a staggering claim is built. If the resurrection of Jesus actually happened, then it is certainly 'the greatest thing in history'. If not, then 20 centuries of Christianity have been built on an error. However attractive the Christian faith may appear as a moral code, there is something hugely unsatisfactory about concluding that it is founded on a delusion or a deception or something worse. This matter, more than any other, deserves our serious attention.

Surely resurrection is unscientific!

Well yes, it probably is. But only in a very narrow sense. It is true that our normal experience is that people die and don't come back to life. It is only natural that we are sceptical of any claim to the contrary. The question is whether there can there be exceptions to the general rule.

Scientific conclusions, as we have seen in an earlier chapter, are based on many observations and the patterns which emerge from them. No scientific theory is set absolutely in stone for all time. New facts come to light which lead to the alteration or even the abandonment of a scientific theory. Scientists are always aware that they may not have the full picture and that some as-yet-unknown factor may alter their conclusions.

We have also noted in a previous chapter that scientific knowledge is not only incomplete in this sense, but it is also limited to certain areas of human experience. There are very real features of human experience which defy scientific explanation. This is not in any sense to diminish the importance or power of modern science, but it is to recognise that there are some matters that are simply beyond its reach.

So, confronted with the claim of the resurrection of Jesus, the most a scientist can say is that it is outside all normal experience. What can't be said, from a scientific point of view, is that it could never happen. How could a scientist possibly know that? What kind of exception to the general rule or what extension of the normal pattern of living and dying could apply in this case is simply not known or perhaps not even knowable scientifically. And if the scientific conclusion is that the resurrection of Jesus must lie beyond normal experience, then that is precisely what Christians have always believed it is!

It's a matter for the historians

If the validity of the resurrection of Jesus cannot be properly assessed by the scientific method, we need to take another approach. In fact we should consider the evidence in the same way as we would for any other event in the past – by the normal methods of historical analysis.

You'd be astonished to find how little solid evidence there is for some historical facts whose accuracy is never questioned. Some of what we learn as solid fact is nothing of the kind and is merely inferred from a few shreds of evidence. So, how much historical evidence is there for something as controversial as the resurrection of Jesus? Well, you'd be surprised!

Clearly, there are only two possibilities. Either the resurrection of Jesus happened as described in the New

Testament or it did not. A good way to approach the evidence is to consider what you would expect to find for the resurrection if it actually happened. Some people, of course, will maintain that something like this could never happen and so refuse to be convinced by any amount of evidence. But if the Christian message is true and God revealed himself to the world in Jesus and validated this by his resurrection, what would it take to convince you? Or could you simply never be convinced? A bit like saying, 'I've made up my mind, don't confuse me with the facts'!

The answer to what it should take to convince you is surprisingly simple. As for any other controversial event, we can only seek the normal historical proofs. These include documentation written by those who witnessed or who were close to the event in point of time. In addition, we would want to see some substantial evidence of the impact of the event on subsequent history. And that is precisely what we have. Although no one actually saw the moment of the resurrection of Jesus, several people witnessed the empty tomb and subsequently encountered him in a variety of settings. They either wrote about the event or were the source from which other writers gained their information. In addition, the various accounts, though differing in the amount of detail they contain – a point which, incidentally, adds to their authenticity – are wholly consistent.

Luke wrote a major part of the history of Jesus and the early church[5] and provides an excellent example of the painstaking and careful writing which characterises the New Testament story. Described as 'our dear friend Luke, the doctor',[6] he was a close companion of Paul and accompanied him for a substantial part of his missionary travels.[7] No one had more opportunity to discuss with the leading figures the dramatic events on which Christianity is built or, on at least one visit to Jerusalem with Paul,[8] to talk to the original disciples and their relatives. Luke's claim to have 'carefully investigated everything from the beginning' and to have found 'many convincing proofs' is wholly credible.[9] His work, along with that of the other writers of the New Testament, is unquestionably worthy of a place on the same shelf as the serious historians of the world.

Beyond all reasonable doubt

Once you set aside any presuppositions you bring to the authenticity of the resurrection of Jesus, you find that the historical evidence is impressive. In summary, it is as follows.

- Firstly, there is the discovery that the tomb of Jesus was empty on the third day after the crucifixion.[10] This was particularly surprising given the fact that a large stone had been used to seal the tomb and a Roman guard mounted to prevent any interference with it.[11] The authorities were clearly afraid that the tomb might be disturbed and had taken steps to stop it. What happened was so embarrassing and unexpected that the guards were later bribed to say that Jesus' disciples had come and stolen the body while they were asleep.[12] A side issue, of course, is how these guards would have known what happened while they were sleeping!

- Secondly, the disciples who first entered the tomb, though completely unsure about what had happened, sensed that something highly unusual had occurred. One of them saw that the grave clothes of Jesus were largely undisturbed – an observation hardly consistent with the forceful removal of the body or the possibility that Jesus had revived in the coolness of the tomb. In fact, one of the disciples who entered the tomb was so impressed with the configuration of Jesus' grave clothes that he immediately sensed a miracle had occurred.[13] It is recorded simply that 'He saw and believed' – and that was before he actually met Jesus in person after the resurrection!

- Thirdly, there are the occasions on which Jesus appeared to his disciples and others, starting from the Sunday of the resurrection until quite some time later. These are sufficiently numerous to merit a summary list as shown in Table 3 below.[14]

  The striking thing about these appearances is that Jesus was seen by individuals and groups, of both men and women at different places and at various times of the day. He ate with some of them; he walked with others; and in most cases he vanished as quickly as he came. Some of the disciples recognised him immediately; others did not know him at first. But they were all agreed that the person they had encountered alive after the crucifixion was unquestionably the same Jesus they had known in the years before.

  These various appearances of Jesus are sometimes dismissed as wishful thinking, hallucinations or some similar illusion experienced by people under extreme emotional pressure. But far from the resurrection stretching our credulity, it really takes some imagination to believe that so many people in so many different circumstances could have shared the same illusion. In fact, as noted earlier, the minor differences in their accounts of what happened actually strengthen their credibility.

- Fourthly, there is the absolutely astonishing transformation in the disciples of Jesus. The men who were too scared to stay with Him when he was crucified and who fled for their lives were somehow turned into lion-like characters. They were convinced Jesus had returned in resurrection to them and they spent the rest of their lives fulfilling His commission to take the gospel into the whole world. Their preaching and teaching gave the world moral teaching of the highest calibre. They suffered persecution and imprisonment almost everywhere they went and were not dissuaded from confronting the pagan culture of their world. Almost all of them experienced cruel and miserable deaths as brave martyrs for the truth.

Now this is not the kind of response you expect from deluded or dishonest fanatics who had cobbled together a wild story about what happened after Jesus' crucifixion. None of it is consistent with a 'conjuring trick with bones', which one bishop so unhelpfully used in recent times to describe the resurrection.

The absolute certainty that the first Christians shared about the resurrection of Jesus is vividly illustrated by the comment made by St Paul in a catalogue of his appearances.[15] He mentions a meeting Jesus had with 500 people at once and adds, with what J.B. Phillips once called 'the ring of truth', that at the time of writing most were 'still alive', thereby implicitly inviting the readers to check for themselves! You simply don't write in that way if you have any doubt about what you are saying.

If you are inclined to think that the evidence for the resurrection of Jesus is flimsy, it is worth researching some of the evidence for other major historical events. By comparison, the evidence for the resurrection of Jesus is overwhelming. The late William Barclay, Professor of New Testament at the University of Glasgow, was surely right when he concluded that the resurrection of Jesus is one of 'the best attested facts of history.'

Table 3: The appearances of Jesus after his resurrection

To whom	When and Where	Bible Reference
Mary Magdalene	Sunday at the tomb	Mark 16:9-11 John 20:11-18
2 travellers	Sunday midday on the road to Emmaus	Luke 24:13-32
Peter	Sunday in Jerusalem	Luke 24:34 1 Corinthians 15:5
10 disciples	Sunday In the upper room	Luke 24:36-43, John 20:19-25
11 disciples	A week later Upper room	John 20:26-31
7 disciples	One day at daybreak while fishing on the Sea of Galilee	John 21:1-23
11 disciples	Some time later on a mountain in Galilee	Matthew 28:16-20 Mark 16:15-18
More than 500	Some time later	1 Corinthians 15:6
James	Some time later	1 Corinthians 15:7
Disciples and others	40 days later, at the Ascension of Jesus into Heaven	Luke 24:44-49 Acts 1:3-8
Paul	Some considerable time later on the road to Damascus	Acts 9:1-19 1 Corinthians 15:8,9

There must be another explanation

Those who dispute or deny the resurrection of Jesus are really obliged to come up with some other explanation of the claim that lies at the heart of Christianity. And some ingenious attempts have been made!

One suggestion is that Jesus did not actually die on the cross but fell into a deep faint and revived in the cool of the tomb. You would have to say that avoiding death during crucifixion, when the soldiers regularly used their spears to ensure the victim had been dispatched, would have been a tricky business. Pulling himself together in a cold tomb, rolling back the stone which sealed the tomb, tip-toeing past the Roman guards, travelling the many miles back to Galilee from Jerusalem and, in his dishevelled state, convincing people who knew him well that he had conquered death and was alive for ever more, would certainly take some doing! And of course, all that makes Jesus the ultimate hoaxer.

Another solution proposes that Jesus' disciples stole his dead body, hid it carefully where no one would find it and then embarked on the biggest deception of all time. Apart from the sheer difficulty of pulling this off under the noses of the ever watchful Roman authorities, this explanation requires us to believe that the 12 apostles, who gave the world the highest kind of moral teaching and almost all of whom died as martyrs for their faith, were no better than a bunch of disreputable fraudsters.

It is surely worth noting, too, that if the Roman or Jewish authorities could have produced the body of Jesus and ended the spread of the message that he had risen again, they certainly would have done so. Christianity was fast becoming a huge pain in their administrative necks! There just was no body to produce!

In a strange way, the alternative explanations for the empty tomb of Jesus greatly strengthen the case for believing. They are just so fantastic as to be truly unbelievable. It is much better to believe the miraculous than to accept the ridiculous!

Is that it?

Well, there is more. While careful historical analysis of the claim that Jesus rose from the dead points overwhelmingly in the direction that it actually happened, there is another strand of evidence. Admittedly this is more subjective, but it follows logically from belief in the resurrection. If Jesus rose from the dead and ascended into heaven as the Bible claims, then he is still alive and can be encountered today. Certainly not in the way the first disciples met him after the resurrection, but no less impressively in the worship and fellowship of the church and in the quiet of personal devotions. I would not expect someone who is sceptical of the claims of the Christian message to accept this point immediately. But when individuals feel the touch of Christ on their lives, they will be assured that everything they have committed themselves to in believing that Jesus was crucified and rose again is undeniably true.

So what then?

The message about Jesus and the resurrection is unquestionably good news. Nevertheless, some of the sophisticated philosophers who first heard it sneered at it[16] and others still do. For Paul, the great defender of the gospel, the implications of the resurrection of Jesus are obvious. His great discourse on resurrection is contained in the New Testament, in 1 Corinthians 15. And the heart of his message is summarised in one statement there. As the New Living Bible puts it

But *the fact is* that Christ has risen from the dead and become the firstfruits of those who have fallen asleep.

(v. 20 – my italic emphasis)

His argument is that

- There is no doubt that the resurrection of Jesus is an historical fact and that all Christian teaching flows from that single, central truth.
- Because Jesus died and rose again, those who believe in him die (or to use the very Christian phrase 'fall asleep') in the secure knowledge that he has gone before them and waits for them.
- The resurrection of Jesus is the guarantee that the future of the world belongs to him and that all those who believe in him will eventually be united with him and with each other at the Great Resurrection at the end of time.

When our two children were small, like all parents find, it was often a great challenge to get them to go to sleep. Every dodge was employed to delay the time when they had to go to bed. And after many songs and stories, and despite overpowering tiredness, they would still fight to resist the coming of sleep. But when it came, their struggles gave way to beautiful and silent slumber. And when they woke up in the morning, if you could beat them to it, it was occasionally possible to see them open their eyes, experience a momentary flicker of anxiety until they saw a face they recognised, and then feel secure in a new day.

That the Christian faith allows such a picture to be used to describe dying is quite awesome. It will, of course, always be a struggle to 'fall asleep' in this final sense, but the ultimate wonder will be to awake in another world where Jesus is and where he shares the power of his resurrection with us.

Next time you hear these words of Jesus, sadly probably only at a funeral, try to grasp their profound meaning.

> I am the resurrection and the life. He who believes in me will
> live, even though he dies; and whoever lives and believes in
> me will never die.

And Jesus added this word for all of us, 'Do you believe this?'[17]

1

Notes

1   See, for example, Bible, New Testament, 1 Cor. 15:12-20.
2   See, for example, Bible, New Testament, Jn. 20:24-31.
3   Bible, New Testament, 1 Cor. 15:17.
4   See, for example, Bible, New Testament, Rom. 1:1-17 and 1 Thes. 4:13-18.
5   See in the New Testament of the Bible, The Gospel according to Luke and The Acts of the Apostles.
6   Bible, New Testament, Col. 4:12.
7   See, for example, Bible, New Testament, Acts 16:10; 2 Tim. 4:11.
8   Bible, New Testament, Acts 21:17 ff.
9   Bible, New Testament, Luke 1: 1-4; Acts 1:1-5.
10   Bible, New Testament, Mt. 28:1-10; Mk. 16:1-8; Lk. 24:1-12; Jn. 20:1-9.
11   Bible, New Testament, Mt. 27:65,66.
12   Bible, New Testament, Mt. 28:11-15.
13   Bible, New Testament, Jn. 20:1-9.
14   Based on information contained in the *New International Version Study Bible*, Hodder & Stoughton, (1985) p. 1556.
15   Bible, New Testament, 1 Cor. 15:1-7.
16   See, for example, Bible, New Testament, Acts 17:18,32.
17   Bible, New Testament, Jn. 11:25,26.

The problem of pain

Alastair Noble

The major news story of the week in which this chapter was written in early 2004 was of the devastating earthquake in the ancient city of Bam in Iran. Described as the world's worst earthquake in decades, the story unfolded predictably, with initial reports of scores of dead, then hundreds and eventually thousands. The graphic pictures of devastated buildings, shattered families, traumatised children and mass graves were all too familiar. Nature, whose beauty is so often impressive, suddenly turned ugly. As onlookers, we shared the sense of helplessness. Our desire to assist could only be given expression by contributing to a relief fund. Even that posed some problems when it was discovered that local laws forbade the import of used clothes. And sadly, but predictably, the earthquake soon gave way to the next big story.

At a personal level, we are occasionally confronted with suffering in a more immediate and enduring way. Someone we know is killed in a road accident; a loved one dies slowly and painfully from a wasting disease; or a child who is dear to us develops a life-threatening illness.

And it is not only suffering that troubles us. There is real evil in the world. The slaughter of innocent children by King Herod in biblical times, the horrors of the slave trade a few centuries ago, and the extermination of six million Jews by the Nazis in the twentieth century are only a few examples from the massive catalogue of misery which is a recurring feature of human history. It is not surprising that we are profoundly disturbed by all this and at a level that challenges religious faith in a kind and loving Creator.

J.W. Wenham is surely right when he insists that evil constitutes the biggest single argument against the existence of an almighty, loving God.[1] You cannot ignore the feeling of people like Edward Tabash, the American lawyer who became a passionate atheist after losing two of his family in the Holocaust, when he said, 'If the God of the Bible actually exists, I want to sue him for negligence, for being asleep at the wheel of the universe when my grandfather and uncle were gassed in Auschwitz.'[2]

A simple statement of the problem is that if God is loving, he cannot be all-powerful. If he is all-powerful, he cannot be loving. But, as we shall see, these propositions are deceptively oversimplified.

Could pain be good for us?

At first sight, such a suggestion seems weird. But in any discussion of pain and suffering, it is easily forgotten that they can be of considerable benefit to us. For example, I have known a few people who suffered from a type of paralysis which removed feeling from some of their limbs and they were in constant danger of serious burns and injuries. If our nervous system did not react with pain when we expose parts of our bodies to physical damage, we would not survive for long. Or sometimes a bitter emotional experience becomes a turning point in our lives and we are able later to look back on it and acknowledge that it had become almost a blessing to us.

While none of this gets near to tackling the central issue, it is one consideration. Indeed, as we shall see later, the ability of God to bring ultimate good out of current evil is part of the Christian hope in the face of suffering.

Confusion and illusion

Christians frequently feel on the defensive when confronted with the problem of pain and evil. But there are two points to make about this. First, Christians are not alone in tackling this dilemma. R.C. Sproul points out that every philosophical system has to deal with these realities in some way.[3] Second, as we have seen in earlier chapters, the complete answers to the fundamental questions of our existence are not accessible by reason alone. We should not be surprised, then, if the ultimate solution to the puzzle of suffering and evil lies beyond our ability to explain it.

Steve Kumar, a leading New Zealand Christian apologist, has given a helpful summary of the various explanations for suffering which are given from the perspective of different world views.[4] He points out that when atheists argue that the presence of evil in the world is incompatible with the nature of God's existence they are engaging in confused thinking. What they claim is that in permitting evil God is guilty of breaking an absolute principle of justice. But there are two problems with this. Firstly, where does this absolute principle of justice come from if there is no God? In atheism, there can be no absolutes of this kind and it is a bit rich to try to argue from one! And, secondly, the existence of evil may well be part of a greater framework of justice which we cannot presently understand. It is, frankly, a bit arrogant to imagine that we have so completely understood the nature of justice and evil that we can pass sentence on God's apparent inaction. In addition, F.J. Sheed makes these telling points about atheism: 'Suffering would be altogether intolerable if there were no God ... Atheism answers that the fact of suffering proves that there is no God. But this does not reduce the world's suffering by one hair-breadth; it only takes away hope'.[5]

In Kumar's treatment, pantheism fares little better! Its approach, he claims, is not confusion but illusion! Some of the religions of the East respond to the problem by essentially denying its existence. The founder of Christian Science, Mary Baker Eddy, follows this line and goes so far as to say, 'Evil is but an illusion, and it has no real basis. Evil is a false belief'.[6] Kumar notes that even Shakespeare wrote, 'There is nothing either good or bad, but thinking makes it so.'[7]

Regarding evil as an illusion is, to any right thinking person, just an evasion of the truth. The slaves of the Southern States or the victims of Hitler's holocaust would not be greatly impressed. I think they would have said it all felt real enough to them. Sigmund Freud's conclusion is inescapable: 'It would be nice if it were true that no evil existed, but the very fact that men wish it to be so makes it highly suspect.'[8] Another consideration is that if evil is merely illusory, there is little incentive to try to improve the lot of those who suffer. This explanation for evil has all the hallmarks of an intellectual and practical cul-de-sac.

Some sources of suffering

A more productive line of inquiry is to try to identify some of the causes of human suffering. And when we try to do so, we discover that there is not a single, simple answer.

Self-inflicted suffering

Although this is not a popular line of explanation, it is one which must be faced. I read recently that at least half of the people who smoke will die of lung cancer – a mountain of suffering which is easily avoidable. If we all drove a little more slowly, refused to drink and drive, observed the speed limits, always used seat belts and child safety seats, and serviced our cars when required, we could certainly save some of the ten or so lives which are lost every day on British roads. If we ate more sensibly, drank less alcohol, took a little exercise regularly and reduced our level of stress, we would significantly improve our health.

There is no doubt that God gets the blame for a great deal of personal misery which is eminently avoidable if we exercised a greater degree of discipline in our way of life.

Carelessness and corruption

It seems harsh to say this, but carelessness and laziness often lie at the root of catastrophic incidents. If we all took a little more time to run through the safety procedures and double-checked anything that looks suspicious, the potential for accidents would be greatly reduced. Understandably, the occasional attempts by pilots to take control of aircraft after consuming alcohol grab the headlines, but they illustrate a deep-seated propensity we all have to imagine that somehow we can avoid the inevitable consequences of our careless actions.

I read some time ago that after a devastating earthquake in a city in South America, it was discovered that the construction of many of the modern buildings were defective. Designed to withstand earthquakes, they had been fatally weakened by concrete which contained too little cement because of the corrupt practices of the builders. Often behind apparent acts of God lie some very human sins.

Selfishness

Much of the misery we inflict on ourselves and others is avoidable. For example, the emotional trauma for children of marital disharmony is often traceable to the selfishness of one or both parents. Or, while 'just wars' sometimes have to be fought, most military conflicts are avoidable and are often fuelled by considerations as diverse as the arrogant selfishness of dictators and the financial interests of arms dealers. The reasons for many wars are not at all mysterious; often they have all too obvious human causes.

Christian perspectives

It is, of course, very easy to sound smug about all this and to suggest that all suffering is avoidable. It certainly is not, and Christians recognise three further dimensions.

- Firstly, there are many examples of catastrophic disasters which have no obvious human cause. Volcanoes, earthquakes, tornados and epidemics are among the dangers humans face and which appear to be part of the natural order. The Christian has to acknowledge that such tragedies are among the mysteries of the world as God has created it.
- Secondly, Christian doctrine teaches that there is a sinister side to evil and suffering. It is not hard to see that in much of the misery and destruction human beings

have inflicted on each other there is something truly demonic. We are often forced to ask how otherwise sensible human beings can get caught up, for example, in acts of murder, genocide and mass destruction such as have been witnessed in Africa, Europe and South East Asia within the last half century. Christians believe that there is an other-worldly force at work – that Satan and his forces of darkness do operate in the world. If you are inclined to be dismissive of that thought, ponder C.S. Lewis' famous comment that the devil's neatest trick is to pretend he does not exist.

- Thirdly, and fundamentally, Christians believe the world is the way it is because of 'original sin' which entered the world at 'the fall' of humankind at the beginning of time. That event, which involved open defiance of God's instructions, brought the suffering and death into the world which touches each of our lives directly and indirectly. Suffering and evil, then, become constant reminders that neither we nor our world are as God intended them to be and that this has been the result of a deliberate human choice.[9]

It is on that third point that Murdo Macdonald makes these powerful observations: 'That original sin is a stubborn and ineradicable fact any one with a knowledge of history is bound to admit. It is not just the individual that is wrong. He is born into a world of disorder that infects him from the first, shaping his thoughts and conditioning most of his reflexes. The doctrine of original sin is not a strain on a reasonable man's credulity.' And he continues, 'It is not part but the totality of man's being that is affected by sin. His will and intellect and emotions are infected by this disease and even the purest of human graces can become the instrument of an evil which permeates the whole of our morbid existence.'[10]

Nevertheless, beyond all the rational and theological explanations, as William Dyrness has pointed out, there remains an underlying and unexplained mystery about the existence of evil and suffering in the universe. That does not mean, however, that Christianity does not have a theology of suffering.

The fixed points

I have occasionally had to drive in fog for so long that I completely lost my bearings and sense of direction. It's a very uncomfortable experience which, in some forms of transport, can be fatal. The only way I know to find out where I am is to look out for something I recognise and set my route from it.

So it is with problem of pain. We cannot deny the challenge it poses and our limitations in trying to explain it. But we need to set it against the things about which we are certain and which are not affected by it. Just as a sailor in a storm will be guided by the familiar points he recognises on the land, or, more likely now, by the unerring electronic navigation systems he uses, so a Christian sets suffering in the wider context of what God has revealed about himself.

- Firstly, the existence of evil and suffering in no way lessens the mystery and magnificence of the universe we inhabit. Everything that underlines the beauty of the world and the security of human relationships is still there. None of it is any less real because of evil and suffering. A close friend may be dying of cancer, but the sun still rises each day in splendid colour and warmth and the birds still sing. Although the problem of pain may make my faith falter, I still have to account for all the beauty and complexity.

- Secondly, I still have a deep moral sense within. Indeed it is that very sense that causes my outrage about the evil and suffering I perceive in the world in the first place. I still have to account for the origin of that moral sense. It is no less acute because I see great imperfections and injustices in the world I inhabit.
- Thirdly, everything that leads me to faith is still relevant. The existence of the material world which compels belief in a Creator has not been removed. The phenomena which cause me to sense God's presence are still there. The reliability of the Bible has not been invalidated. And most crucially, the historic certainty of the resurrection of Jesus Christ has not been diminished.

Christian teaching about suffering and evil

It becomes apparent to the believer that the problem of suffering and evil has to be set within the wider framework of faith which, as we have seen in previous chapters, recognises the limits of reason and rationality. Just as we cannot fully understand by intellectual effort alone the existence of God and the nature of the world he has created, so we find that the origin and nature of suffering eludes our precise analysis.

Stated simply then, the Christian believes that God knows what he is doing, even in permitting evil and suffering to invade his universe. If you are inclined to reject this view, it is worth asking if there is any other explanation which does justice to all the factors which bear on the matter.

In conclusion, then, it may be helpful to summarise the distinctly Christian teaching on evil and suffering which come from what God has revealed to us through his word, the Bible.

1   It is part of the wonder of our humanity that God has entrusted us with freedom of choice, even to the point of allowing us to defy his will and cause suffering to ourselves and others. To have denied us this freedom might have been a safer option, but it would have created some kind of humanoid robot, incapable of independent decision and action.[11]

2   By defying God's word, we have fallen into sin, the consequences of which have affected every aspect of our lives. To restore our relationship with God, we need to repent of our sin. Only through faith in the sacrifice of Christ on the cross can we find forgiveness. By opening our lives to the Holy Spirit through that same faith in Christ we can find the strength to resist temptation and wrongdoing.[12]

3   The ultimate struggle between good and evil lies beyond this world and stems from a deep rebellion in celestial spheres. Satan or the devil is a real person who has defied the Almighty and has enlisted a host of fallen angels to do his dirty work in the world. This is the position which Jesus and the apostles clearly taught. The only sure refuge from such satanic influence is the saving power of Jesus Christ.[13]

4   For reasons best known to himself, God often works through his Holy Spirit in our suffering. He sanctifies it and can make it a blessing to us and, through us, to others. Suffering, more than prosperity and plenty, is likely to produce patience, perseverance and character.[14]

5   God often chooses to compensate us for what we suffer. This is not the invariable rule and the recompense for suffering may be delayed until the world to come. Then all wrongs will be righted and those who caused suffering will answer to God for their actions.[15]

6   Most remarkably of all, God chose in the person of Jesus Christ to enter into our suffering. And not just the normal suffering of human experience, but the ultimate pain of wrongful execution by crucifixion. That Christ should suffer to such a degree brings sacredness to suffering and a clear sense that he understands our struggles.[16]

7   The resurrection of Jesus establishes his permanent victory over evil and proclaims the certainty that, when he comes again, he will establish his Kingdom of Righteousness for ever and make an end of all suffering.[17] This is the enduring hope of the Christian church which it has carried across the centuries and into every experience of pain and persecution.

The suffering of Christ

In his excellent booklet about the events of 11 September 2001 in New York, John Blanchard quotes some powerful words which were first written in the 1960s.[18] It is appropriate to reproduce them here.

At the end of time, billons of people were scattered on a great plain before God's throne. Most shrank from the brilliant light before them. But some groups near the front talked heatedly – not with cringing shame but with belligerence. 'Can God judge us?' – they shouted

'How can He know about suffering?' snapped a pert young brunette. She ripped open a sleeve to reveal a tattooed number from a Nazi concentration camp. 'We endured terror…beating…torture…death!' In another group a black man lowered his collar. 'What about this,' he demanded, showing an ugly rope burn. 'Lynched for no crime but being black!' In another crowd, there was a pregnant schoolgirl with sullen eyes. 'Why should I suffer?' she murmured, 'It wasn't my fault.'

Far out across the plain were hundreds of such groups. Each had a complaint against God for the evil and suffering he had permitted in the world. How lucky God was to live in heaven where all was sweetness and light, where there was no weeping or fear, no hunger or hatred! What did God know of all that people had been forced to endure in this world? 'For God leads a pretty sheltered life,' they said.

So each of these groups sent forth their leader, chosen because he had suffered the most. A Jew, a black, a person from Hiroshima, a horribly disabled arthritic, a thalidomide child. In the centre of the plain they consulted with each other.

At last they were ready to present their case. It was rather clever. Before God could be qualified to be their Judge, he must endure what they had endured. The verdict was that God should be sentenced to live on earth – as a man! Let him be born a Jew. Let the legitimacy of his birth be doubted. Give him a work so difficult that even his family will think him out of his mind when he tries to do it. Let him be betrayed by his closest friends. Let him face false charges, be tried by a preju-diced jury and convicted by a cowardly judge. Let him be tor-tured. At last, let him see what it means to be terribly alone. Then let him die in agony. Let him die so that there can be no doubt that he has died. Let there be a whole host of witnesses to verify it.

As each leader announced the portion of his sentence, a loud murmur of approval went up from the throng of people assembled. When the last had finished pronouncing sen-tence there was a long silence. No one uttered another word. No one moved. For suddenly all knew that God had already served his sentence.

Finally faith

William Dyrness has made this following comment which summarises the position of a believer: 'It is a Christian conviction that evil can be used in a higher purpose, that suffering produces saintliness. If this is true, then it is possible that God's unwillingness to create a world in which evil is impossible reflects neither on His goodness or on His power, but flows from His eternal and unchanging purposes ... Perhaps when we view creation in its totality, we will see evil as a necessary element in the meaning of the whole.'[19] Actually, there is no other tenable position!

Let the last word on this topic go to St Paul. In the historic passage which sparked the Protestant Reformation of the sixteenth century, he goes to the very heart of the Christian message with its focus on the need for personal faith in Jesus Christ.

> Therefore, since we have been justified through faith, we have peace with God through our LORD Jesus Christ, through whom we have gained access by faith into this grace in which we now stand. And we rejoice in the hope of the glory of God. Not only so, but we also rejoice in our sufferings, because we know that suffering produces perseverance; perseverance, character; and character, hope. And hope does not disappoint us, because God has poured out his love into our hearts by the Holy Spirit, whom he has given us.[20]

Notes

1 John W. Wenham, 'Response', in Geisler, *The Roots of Evil* p. 89. See also, Wenham's book *The Goodness of God.*

2 Quoted by John Blanchard in *Where was God on September 11ᵗʰ?* (Evangelical Press, 2002).

3 R.C. Sproul, *Objections Answered*, p. 131.

4 S. Kumar, *Christianity for Sceptics*, especially chapter 2.

5 Quoted by S. Kumar, *Christianity for Sceptics.*

6 Mary Baker Eddy, *Science and Health with Key to the Scriptures* p. 480.

7 Hamlet, Act 2, scene 2, line 225.

8 N.L. Geisler *Philosophy of Religion*, p. 312.

9 See for example, Bible, Old Testament, Gen. 3; New Testament, Rom. 5:12-21.

10 Murdo Macdonald, *The Need to Believe*, p. 56.

11 See, for example, Bible, Old Testament, Gen. 2:15-17; New Testament, Rom. 1:24-27.

12 Bible, New Testament, Rom. 5:12-21.

13 See, for example, Bible, New Testament, Lk. 10:17-20; 2 Pet. 2:4-10; Rom. 16:20; 1 Pet. 5:8-11.

14 See, for example, Bible, New Testament, Rom. 5:3-5.

15 See, for example, Bible, New Testament, Mt. 16:24-28; Mk. 10:29,30; 2 Cor. 4:16-18.

16 See, for example, Bible, New Testament, Phil. 2:5-11; 1 Pet. 2:21.

17 See, for example, Bible, New Testament, 1 Cor. 15:20-28.

18 John Blanchard, *Where was God on September 11ᵗʰ?*

19 William Dyrness, *Christian Apologetics in a World Community*, p. 155.

20 Bible, New Testament, Rom. 5:1-5.

Bibliography

Baker, David W. (ed.), *Looking into the Future* (Baker, 2001)

Blanchard, John, *Where was God on September 11th?* (Evangelical Press, 2002)

Brown, Colin, *Philosophy and the Christian Faith* (IVP, 1969)

Bruce, F.F., *Jesus and Christian Origins Outside the New Testament* (Hodder & Stoughton, 1984)

Bruce, F.F., *The New Testament Documents: Are they Reliable?* (Eerdmans, 1983)

Clark, Robert E.D., *Darwin, Before and After* (The Paternoster Press, 1948)

Copley, Terence, *About the Bible* (Bible Society, 1990)

Craig, William Lane, *Apologetics: An Introduction* (Moody Press, 1984)

Crick, Francis, *Life Itself* (New York: Simon and Schuster, 1981)

Crick, Francis and L.E. Orgel, *Directed Panspermia* (Icarus, 1973).

Dawkins, Richard, *The Blind Watchmaker* (Penguin, 1986)

Denton M., *Evolution: A Theory in Crisis* (Adler and Adler, 1986)

Dyrness, William, *Christian Apologetics in a World Community* (IVP, 1983)

Eddy, Mary Baker, *Science and Health with Key to the Scriptures* (Boston: The First Church of Christ Scientist, 1994)

Edwards, Paul (ed.), *Encyclopaedia of Philosophy*, Vol.5

Encyclopaedia Britannica (2003)

Geisler, Norman and Peter Bocchino, *Unshakable Foundations* (Bethany House, 2001)

Geisler, Norman and William E. Nix, A *General Introduction to the Bible* (Moody, 1986)

Geisler, Norman, *Christian Apologetics* (Baker, 2002)

Geisler, N. (ed), *The Roots of Evil* (Zondervan, 1978)

Gould, Stephen Jay, *Wonderful Life* (New York: W.W. Norton, 1989)

Hume, David, (ed. Chas Hendel) *An Enquiry Concerning Human Understanding* (New York: Liberal Arts Press, 1955)

Johnson, Phillip E., *Darwin on Trial* (IVP, 1991).

Johnson, Phillip E., *Wedge of Truth* (IVP, 2000)

Kenyon, Frederic G., *Our Bible and the Ancient Manuscripts* (New York: Harper, 1958)

Kumar, Steve, *Christianity for Sceptics* (John Hunt Publishing, 2000)

Lewis, C.S., *Mere Christianity* (Fontana, 1952)

Lewis, C.S., *Miracles* (New York: Macmillan, 1960).

Little, Paul E., *Know Why you Believe* (IVP, 2000)

Macdonald, Murdo, *The Need to Believe* (Fontana, 1959)

McDowell, Josh, *The New Evidence that Demands a Verdict* (Nelson, 1999)

Mackean, D.G., *Life Study, A Textbook of Biology* (John Murray, 1981)

McKinnon, Alastair, 'Miracles' and 'Paradox' (*American Philosophical Quarterly* 4, October 1967)

Metzger, Bruce, *The Text of the New Testament* (Clarendon Press, 1968)

Milton R., *The Facts of Life* (Corgi, 1992)

Moreland, J.P., *Scaling the Secular City* (Baker, 2001)

Ramm, Bernard, *Protestant Christian Evidences* (Chicago: Moody Press, 1953)

Sproul, R.C., *Objections Answered* (Glendale, California: G/L Publishing, 1978)

Stott, John, *The Incomparable Christ* (IVP, 2001)

Strobel, Lee, *The Case for Faith* (Zondervan, 2000)

Tucker, Ruth, *Strange Gospels* (Marshall Pickering, 1989)
Vermes, Geza, *The Authentic Gospel of Jesus* (Penguin, 2003)
Wells, Jonathan, *Icons of Evolution, Science or Myth?* (Regnery, 2000)
Wenham, John, *The Goodness of God* (IVP, 1974)

www.answeringenesis.org/doc/1342
www.statistics.gov.uk